STUDIES IN ENGLISH LITERATURE

Volume XIV

JOHN CROWNE'S
SIR COURTLY NICE
A CRITICAL EDITION

by

CHARLOTTE BRADFORD HUGHES

1966

MOUTON & CO.

THE HAGUE · PARIS

Printed in The Netherlands.

ACKNOWLEDGMENTS

I should like to acknowledge my gratitude for assistance with this edition of John Crowne's *Sir Courtly Nice* to those who originally directed the project as a doctoral dissertation at Brown University: to the late Professor R. Gale Noyes, the chairman, and to Professors Leicester Bradner and Juan Lopez-Morillas. For their suggestions and encouragement I am also greatly indebted to Professors Oliver M. Willard, Chandler B. Beall, and Perry J. Powers of the University of Oregon, and, for her help in reading and criticizing portions of the text, to Miss Hildegard Weiss of Portland State College.

Particular thanks are due the staff of the Houghton Library at Harvard University, and to those at the University of Oregon Library and the Portland State College Library who kindly made rare books, inter-library loans, and special services available during the preparation of the manuscript.

Portland, Oregon, 1965   C.B.H.

TABLE OF CONTENTS

I. INTRODUCTION

A. THE TEXT

The present text of *Sir Courtly Nice* is based upon the first quarto, 1685, of which sixteen copies are in libraries in the United States.[1] The text has been compared with that of the second quarto, 1693, and with that of the third quarto of 1703, of which there seem to have been two impressions taken from the same type and published and sold by different dealers. Further reprints of the play appeared in 1724, 1731, 1735, 1750, 1758, and 1765. In 1873-74 the play was edited by James Maidment and W. H. Logan for their series entitled *Dramatists of the Restoration,* and in 1922 an edition by Montague Summers appeared with *The Parson's Wedding* and *The London Cuckolds* in *Restoration Comedies.*

George Parker Winship, in his bibliography of Crowne's works,[2] lists the following editions after the first:

(2) [Sir Courtly Nice: or, It cannot Be.] . . .The Second Edition . . . London, Printed by M. B. for R. Bently . . . M.DC.XCIII. 4°. 8, 51, 1 pp.

(3) [The Same.] by Her Majesty's Servants . . . London: Printed for R. Wellington, at the Daulphin at the West-end of St. Pauls; and

---

[1] At the Library of Congress, Folger, Huntington, Newberry, and Boston Public Libraries, and college libraries at Harvard, Yale, Princeton, Brown, Vassar, Michigan, Pennsylvania, Southern California, Virginia, Texas, and Ohio State. Copies in England include those at the British Museum, the Bodleian, and Gray's Inn Libraries.

[2] George Parker Winship, *A Bibliography of The Restoration Dramatist John Crowne* (Cambridge, Mass., 1922).

E. Rumball, at the Post-house in Covent-Garden, 1703. 4°. 8, 64 pp.

(3a) [The Same.] London: Printed for B. Tooke, at the Middle Temple Gate in Fleetstreet, near Temple-Bar; and G. Strahan at the Golden-Ball, overagainst the Royal-Exchange in Cornhill, 1703. 4°. 8, 64 pp. (A change in the position of the catchword on p. 15 shows that the two 1703 editions were separate impressions from the same type.)

(4) [The Same.] . . . As it was Acted . . . London, Printed for G. Strahan, at the Golden-Ball over-against the Royal-Exchange in Cornhill; S. Tooke, and B. Motte, at the Middle-Temple-Gate in Fleetstreet, MDCCXXIV. 12°. 12, 81, 3 pp.

(5) [The Same.] London: Printed for G. Strahan, over against the Royal Exchange in Cornhill; B. Motte, at the Middle-Temple-Gate in Fleetstreet; J. Poulson; and Richard, James, and Bethel Wellington. MDCC.XXXI. 12°. 12, 81, 3 pp.

(6) [The Same.] London, Printed for W. Feales, at Rowe's Head, the Corner of Essex-Street in the Strand; G. Strahan against the Royal Exchange in Cornhill; B. Motte, at the Middle-Temple-Gate in Fleetstreet; R. Wellington, at the Dolphin and Crown, and C. Corbett, at Addison's Head, both without Temple-Barr; and J. Brindley, at the King's Arms in New Bond-strtet. (sic) MDCCXXXV. 12°. 108 pp. Frontispiece 'Arnoldus Vanhaecken invt. et Delin. Aegidius King sculp.' Title in red and black.

(7) [The Same.] As it is Acted at the Theatres-Royal In Drury Lane and Covent Garden, By His Majesty's Servants. Written by Mr. Crown. London: Printed for C. Bathurst, Mess. Hawes, Clarke, and Collins, I. Lowndes, T. Caslon, and C. Corbett. MDCCLXV. 12°. 76 pp.

Winship also lists the following foreign editions of the play:

[The Same.] SIR PHANTAST oder Es kann nicht seyn, Ein Lustspiel in fünf Aufzügen aus dem Englischen des John Crown. Bremen. Bey Johann Heinrich Cramer, 1767. 8°. 4, 164 pp. 1 p. Corrigenda.

[The Same.] Die unmögliche Sache. Ein Lustspiel in vier Aufzügen nach dem Englishchen (sic) des Crown. Aufgefuhrt im k.k. National-Hoftheater. Wien. Zu findenbeym Logenmeister 1782. 8°. 95 pp.

Not included in Winship's bibliography are the following:

(6a) [The Same.] As it was Acted by Her Majesty's Servants. Written by Mr. Crown. London: Printed for G. Strahan; C. Bathurst, over against St. Dunstan's Church in Fleetstreet; and sold by Alexander Strahan, at the Golden Ball in Cornhill. 1750. 12°.

(6b) [The Same.] As it is Perform'd at the Theatres-Royal in London and Dublin, Dublin: Printed by D. Chamberlaine, For Sarah

Cotter, under Dick's Coffee-House in Skinner-Row. MDCC.LVIII. 12°.

In addition, a supplementary *Prologue and Epilogue* to the first edition is described by both Winship and Summers.[3] This is a broadside, printed "for Tho. Benskin *at the Corner Shop in* Little-Lincolns-Inn-Fields. 1685". The Prologue is the same as that of the first quarto, except for minor variants noted below, but the Epilogue is considerably different. Summers believed that the broadside represented the Epilogue as originally delivered in the playhouse, but later "altered and improved".[4]

Sir Courtly Nice appears in the Term Catalogues for Michaelmas term, 1685, as the third entry in the category of Plays, after "A Common-Wealth of Women. By Mr. D'Urefey". Both quartos were priced at one shilling and printed for the same publishers, Bentley and Hindmarsh. The collation of the first edition is as follows:

Sir Courtly Nice:/ or,/ It cannot Be./ A / COMEDY/ As it is Acted by His Majesties/ Servants./ Written by Mr. Crown./ LONDON,/ Printed by *H.H.* Jun. for *R. Bently,* in *Russel-street,*/ Covent-Garden, and *Jos. Hindmarsh,* at the/ *Golden-Ball* over against the *Royal Ex-/change* in Cornhill. M.DC.LXXXV./
4° A-I 2
A, title page; *verso,* The Names of the Persons; A 2 The Epistle Dedicatory; A 3 The Prologue; A 4 Epilogue; B-I 2 text of the play, and A Song; *verso,* A Song.
Pagination at upper right hand corner, *recto,* and upper left, *verso.* [8] 1 [B 1] – 60 [I 2].
Copies used: USC and LC (Micro-print reproduction)
Copies examined: Hvd, Yale, Prin, Mich, Penn, Vas.

All of the eight first quartos examined appear to have been printed from the same type, since the number of peculiarities common to

[3] A copy of this is available in the Houghton Library at Harvard. Summers used an apparently identical copy in his edition, which he found in the British Museum among other theatrical papers. The symbol *1 b* is used in the textual notes to indicate readings from the broadside Prologue and Epilogue.
[4] Summers contended in *The Restoration Theatre* (1934), pp. 13-14, that these broadsides were employed as advertisements during the performance of plays and that the form of the Prologue or Epilogue was frequently changed before publication.

all is considerably greater than the number of differences between them. The Pennsylvania copy (Penn 1) contains the largest number of variant readings, but they are confined to A 2, which appears to have been corrected extensively after the printing of this copy. At the head of that page Penn 1 omits Ormonde's title, "Knight of the Most Noble Order of the Garter", which appears in all other copies and in subsequent editions. It gives bad readings on lines 9, 20, 24, 37, 42, and 49. Apparently the corrections were confined to the single page, however, and not extended to the entire outer forme, since A, A 3, and A 4^v seem to be identical in all copies examined.

The Vassar copy (Vas 1) is remarkable only for the mis-pagination of 52-53. Only the numbers are in error; the pages are in order and are otherwise similar, in such respects as broken dashes, to those of all other copies. The quartos from the Library of Congress (LC 1) and from the library of the University of Southern California (USC 1) seem to be identical in all details, and the Princeton (Prin 1) and Yale copies are like them except for a very few differences of spacing and type face which might be explained by accidental displacement during the printing process. (For example, on G 4^v Princeton, Michigan and Vassar have "Pons" for "pons" in line 1, but all quartos print "brot'her" in line 32.) The Michigan (Mich 1) quarto is like the Harvard (Hvd 1) one in that it prints the better reading "Inchantments" in line 28 of A 2^v where the others have "inclinations".

In editing the text I have followed the policy of silently correcting:

1) turned letters when they do not resemble other letters.

2) omission of period at end of sentence and omission of capital at beginning of sentence or verse line.

3) double punctuation, only one of the marks being retained.

4) uncapitalized pronoun *I*.

5) misprint, as "brot'her" for "brother".

I have standardized stage directions so that

1) first word of direction begins with capital letter.

2) direction ends with period.

3) speaker's name is prefixed to speech.

4) names are consistently italicized.

5) direction describing dialogue precedes it.

In the latter respect, the text is inconsistent, giving such instructions as "Aside" now before, now after, the appropriate dialogue. Directions enclosed in brackets are my own, and are supplied only when they are needed for clarity.

There is no evidence that Crowne assumed responsibility for any printing of the text but the first, although the second and third quartos appeared during his lifetime. I have, however, substituted in the text some readings from the second and third quartos and from the broadside Prologue and Epilogue when they seemed to improve the sense or when a mark of punctuation or a spelling, such as "one" for "own" made possible misreading or mispronunciation.[5] Emendations not indicated by edition number are mine; two are adopted from the edition by Montague Summers cited above. All substitution has been fully annotated at the bottom of the pages. Minor spelling and punctuation changes occurring in editions after the first are not noted, since standardization in these texts is imperfect. Changes involving any alteration of meaning are recorded in the notes.

B. THE LIFE AND DRAMATIC WORKS OF JOHN CROWNE

The most complete and accurate biographical account of John Crowne is the work of Arthur F. White, who, in his monograph *John Crowne: His Life and Dramatic Works* (1922), corrected the older work of A. T. Bartholomew in *The Cambridge History of English Literature* (1912) and that of A. H. Bullen in the *Dictionary of National Biography* (1888). White has established that the playwright Crowne was the son of William Crowne, a member of the household of the Earl of Arundel, who accompanied his patron on an embassy to the court of Ferdinand II of Germany in

---

[5] The copy of the second edition cited is from the Yale Library; the third quarto cited is that from the William Andrews Clark Memorial Library of the University of California at Los Angeles, reproduced on microfilm. Copies of both editions in the Houghton Library at Harvard were also examined.

1636 and published an account of his travels the following year.[6] William Crowne, through the favor of the Earl, became Rouge Dragon in the College of Arms in 1638, and during the Civil War and Commonwealth served as a lieutenant-colonel in the Parliamentary Army. In 1654 he became a Member of Parliament for Bridgnorth, and two years later entered into partnership with Colonel Thomas Temple to become joint proprietor of the province of Nova Scotia. In 1657 Colonel Crowne became sole proprietor of the lesser half of the territory and shortly afterward leased his section, the Penobscot River country, to Temple at an annual rental of £110. Temple, after the first year, refused to pay the rent, although he retained the territory. At the Restoration William Crowne returned to England for the Coronation of Charles II and defended his and Temple's claim to Nova Scotia against others who hoped for a new grant from the king. Although he succeeded in protecting his right to the territory, Temple made no reparation and in 1667 by the treaty of Breda, Nova Scotia was ceded to the French. In 1662 Crowne had returned to New England, where he lived until his death in Boston in 1683.[7]

John Crowne was the eldest of three children born to William and Agnes Mackworth Crowne, whose brother Humphrey had been a member of Cromwell's Council of State. The date of the dramatist's birth is probably 1640, and the place almost certainly Shropshire, the location of the family estate of the Mackworths. John Crowne accompanied his father to America in 1657, and entered Harvard College the same year, boarding in Boston at the home of John Norton, "the teacher of the principal independent church".[8] At the time of Crowne's enrollment at Harvard, the entrance requirement included ability "to understand Tully, or such like Classical Latine author ex tempore, and to make and

---

[6] *A true relation of all the remarkable places and passages observed in the travels of Thomas, Lord Howard, earle of Arundell and Surrey, ambassadour extraordinary to Ferdinando II, 1636.*

[7] Arthur F. White, *John Crowne: His Life and Dramatic Works*, Ch. I, I, "The Playwright's Father", pp. 7-21.

[8] From a deposition by John Crowne in George Chalmers, *Political Annals of the Present United Colonies*, Bk. I, pp. 263-64. Quoted by White, p. 26.

speake true Latine in verse and prose . . . and to decline perfectly
the paradigms of nounes and verbes in the Greek tongue".[9] The
curriculum included natural philosophy, arithmetic, geometry,
astronomy, ethics, politics, logic, Greek, Hebrew, Chaldee, Syriac,
rhetoric, prosody, declamations, disputations, Bible and catechism,
and in concession to the laws of nature, history in winter, botany
in summer. Each student was required to report to his tutor twice
a day, for prayers and for an accounting of his day's reading.
Perhaps it is to be expected that, though Crowne's tragedies show
what White considers "a competent acquaintance" with the classical historians, his works reveal nothing of his early life unless it
is the rejection of the dogma and politics of dissent apparent in
his later acceptance of Tory politics and religious orthodoxy.[10]

The poverty of the Crowne family following the disastrous
American venture may be inferred from the fact that most of
Crowne's adult life was spent in attempting to gain, through royal
favor, restitution for the injustices that his father had suffered.
John Dennis said of Crowne that on his return to England in
1660 "Necessity . . . oblig'd him to become a Gentleman-Usher to
an old Independant Lady. But he soon grew as weary of that
precise Office, as he had been . . . of the Discipline of *Nova
Scotia*".[11] As may be seen from the foregoing, the accuracy of
Dennis is questionable, but Crowne's choice of a literary career
was undoubtedly an attempt to utilize his education in order to
support himself independently. His first literary work was a taste-
less and unpromising prose romance entitled *Pandion and Amphigeneia, or the Coy Lady of Thessalia,* published in 1665, of
which he said, "I was scarce twenty years when I fancied it."[12]
If the poet's memory is correct, the inspiration would date from
1660, the year of his return from America and the period of his

[9] *New England's First Fruits, in respect to the progress of Learning in
the Colledge At Cambridge in Massachusetts-bay* . . . (London, 1643), p. 13.
Quoted by White, p. 25.

[10] White believes that Crowne's anti-Catholic views of later life are the
result of early training in Protestant theology at Harvard.

[11] John Dennis, *The Critical Works,* ed. Edward Niles Hooker, II, 404.

[12] Dedication to *Pandion and Amphigeneia* (1665), quoted by White,
pp. 23-24.

service referred to by Dennis. White remarks that "it is significant that Crowne's entry upon the career of play-writing closely follows his father's loss of the Penobscot estate".[13]

Crowne's dramatic works may be grouped into two classifications, the romantic plays – tragedies, heroic dramas, and his pastoral and romantic comedies – and the satirical comedies. Of these, the first group is much the larger, though not the more interesting to the modern reader. To it belongs Crowne's first play, *Juliana* (1671), a romantic comedy dedicated to the Earl of Orrery and acted "with moderate success" at the Duke of York's Theatre. His second, a rhymed tragedy entitled *The History of Charles the Eighth,* and written the same year, was an improvement upon the confused plotting of his initial effort, and ran for six days at the new theatre in Dorset Garden, with Betterton in the part of Charles VIII. It was printed in 1672, with a dedication to the Earl of Rochester, who proved a somewhat unpredictable patron, for he wrote, perhaps in collaboration with Buckingham, *Timon, a Satyr* in 1673, ridiculing Settle's *Empress of Morocco,* Crowne's *Charles the Eighth* and *Pandion,* and Dryden's *Indian Emperor.* To the preface of Settle's tragedy Dryden, with Crowne and Shadwell, replied in 1674 with the abusive *Notes and Observations on the Empress of Morocco.* Rochester again rebuked Crowne, Settle, and Dryden, among others, in *An Allusion to Horace* (1675). Rochester, with others of the Court Wits, lampooned Crowne once more in *A Session of the Poets* (1676), but Crowne's masque *Calisto* had meanwhile been produced at Court, apparently through the intervention of Rochester. After a quarrel between Rochester and Lord Mulgrave, the latter became Dryden's patron and Rochester Dryden's enemy, taking pleasure in encouraging the poet's rivals, notably Settle, whom Rochester had previously aided. After Settle's popularity had become established, Rochester withdrew his patronage, and when an entertainment was to be ordered for the royal princesses, he interceded with the king in behalf of Crowne. According to Edmond Malone, "by the recommendation of Crowne Rochester's malice was doubly gratified;

---

[13] White, "John Crowne and America", *PMLA,* XXXV (1920), 454. Much of the material from this article was re-used in the later monograph.

for besides mortifying Settle, a marked slight was shown to Dryden, whose office as Poet Laureate it peculiarly was to compose such entertainments for the court".[14] *Calisto* marks the beginning of Crowne's literary relationship with the king, which endured until the end of the reign and promised to reward him richly with *Sir Courtly Nice* until the king's untimely death removed that hope. White remarks that the masque brought Crowne "into the place of prominence in literary circles which Settle had held but recently".[15] Following a success in comedy with *The Countrey Wit* in 1675, Crowne experienced a greater one with the two-part *Destruction of Jerusalem,* acted at the Theatre Royal in 1677 by the King's Company and received with something of the enthusiasm that greeted Settle's *The Empress of Morocco* in 1671. After Crowne's triumph, Rochester, with his characteristic inconsistency, grew jealous and transferred his patronage to Otway. A contemporary account is given in a letter supposedly written by St. Evremond to the Duchess of Mazarin and prefixed to an edition of Rochester's works:

But when Mr. Crowne's 'Destruction of Jerusalem' had met with as wild and unaccountable success as Mr. Dryden's 'Conquest of Granada', his Lordship withdrew his favour as if he would be still in contradiction to the town.[16]

The Ambitious Statesman, a verse tragedy, appeared in 1679, the year that Crowne put to the test the favor he had gained with King Charles as a result of his stage successes by petitioning the king for proprietorship of Mounthope, near the Plymouth settlements, as compensation for the loss of his father's property in Nova Scotia. The request, opposed by the Governor and Council of New Plymouth, was denied, and the play met with unfavorable response. Although Crowne attributed the failure to the malice of his enemies, White ascribes it to unsettled conditions in England, then in an uproar over the Popish Plot.

[14] Edmond Malone, *The Critical and Miscellaneous Prose Works of John Dryden* (London, 1800) I, Part I, 124, as quoted in White, pp. 78-79.
[15] White, p. 34.
[16] Preface to *The Works of the Earl of Rochester, Roscommon, and Dorset* (London, 1731) quoted by Maidment and Logan, *The Dramatic Works of John Crowne,* II, 218.

Prompted by violent political strife and secure in the patronage of Charles II, Crowne now adapted parts of the Shakespearean trilogy of *Henry VI* in two political plays, *The Miseries of Civil War* (1680) and *Henry VI* (1681). Other dramatists had helped to make the London stage at this time a scene of intense political conflict, and Crowne seems to have believed that he could maintain a middle course between the Whig and the Catholic partisans. G. W. Whiting in his article "Political Satire in London Stage Plays, 1680-1683", states that a "Whig offensive" in the theatre occurred in 1680, "bringing a considerable amount of satire upon Catholics and . . . some denunciation of incompetent rulers". *The Miseries of Civil War* Whiting calls the most important loyal play of 1680:

Politically, Crowne's *The Miseries of Civil War* is more important than Otway's play [*The Souldier's Fortune*]. In this version of *Henry the Sixth, Part III,* Crowne has magnified the horrors of civil war and has proclaimed obedience to lawful authority a sacred duty.

However, when in 1681 the "Tory offensive" followed in retaliation, "with emphasis upon the rebellious antecedents and purposes of the Whigs", Crowne chose an inopportune time to introduce *Henry VI* and the tragedy *Thyestes,* both of which contained satire of Catholics.[17] Since this subject had become distasteful to the Court, where the succession of James II was being contemplated, *Henry VI* was suppressed. After satirizing the Whigs in the comedy *City Politiques* (1682) Crowne discovered that his "golden mean" had earned him the enmity of both extreme political factions.

Darius, King of Persia (1688) was Crowne's first drama to be written after the death of Charles II. In the dedication he explains that he would not have "meddled with tragedy" at a time when *Sir Courtly Nice* (1685) had established his success in comedy, had it not been for a "tedious sickness", with which he was afflicted. Despite Crowne's political position, James II attended the third-day performance of *Darius* and helped to make the play a financial, if not a dramatic, success.

[17] G. W. Whiting, "Political Satire in London Stage Plays, 1680-1683", *Modern Philology,* XXVIII (1930), 29-43.

With the death of Charles II, Crowne had given up hope of the restoration of his estates or other compensation from the king, and his religious opinions led him into the party of the Whigs once the Catholics were in power. When his comedy *The English Frier* was suppressed for its anti-Catholic satire, Crowne turned again to serious drama with *Regulus* (1692), called by Genest an "indifferent tragedy". His last tragedy, *Caligula,* was a reversion to the heroic couplet, though not to the heroic theme, and is thus, in White's words, a "literary curiosity".

In the intervals of producing tragedies judged mediocre in his own day, Crowne wrote five comedies which, on the whole, met with greater success during his lifetime and constitute the major interest that their author possesses for the reader of the present. The first of them, *The Countrey Wit,* was written in 1675, after the success of the masque *Calisto,* and was praised by Charles II. It continued on the stage until 1727, being acted at least ten times during the eighteenth century; an indication of its popularity is the fact that a second edition was published in 1693 and a third in 1735. Langbaine pointed out in 1699 that the subplot was a borrowing from Molière's *Le Sicilien, ou L'Amour Peintre.* White gives a detailed account of these borrowings, together with examples of characters and scenes that resemble some in *Tartuffe, Monsieur de Pourceaugnac,* and *Les Femmes Savantes,* but he believes the low-comedy character Sir Mannerly Shallow to be original with Crowne, who had attempted this type of caricature with the Landlord in farce scenes in the romantic comedy *Juliana.* White also finds reminiscences of Etherege and Wycherley in *The Countrey Wit,* and feels that portions of the play belong to the comedy of manners, although the abundance of farce makes Crowne's classification of it as "low comedy" the correct one.

The production of *City Politiques* (1682) was delayed, according to Dennis, because *"Bennet* Lord *Arlington,* who was then Lord Chamberlain of the King's Houshold, and who had secretly espous'd the Whigs who were at that time powerful in Parliament ... us'd all his Authority to suppress it".[18] Nevertheless, when it came to be played it was applauded, and Crowne alludes to its

---

[18] Dennis, II, 405.

"victory" in his preface to the text, which was printed in 1683, and again in 1688. The satire in this play was directed at Lord Shaftesbury, Titus Oates, Stephen Colledge, and other Whig leaders; its topicality, however, did not prevent its being revived in 1705, 1712, and 1717.

Sir Courtly Nice, one of the most popular comedies of the Restoration period, was the outcome of another plea of Crowne to the king for a royal post that would enable him to retire from his professional career as a dramatist. The best and most frequently cited account of its composition is that of Dennis:

It was at the very latter End of King *Charles's* Reign, that Mr. *Crown* being tyr'd with the Fatigue of Writing, and shock'd by the Uncertainty of Theatrical Success, and desirous to shelter himself from the Resentments of those numerous Enemies which he had made by his *City Politicks,* made his Application immediately to the King himself; and desir'd his Majesty to establish him in some Office, that might be a Security to him for Life. The King had the Goodness to assure him, he should have an Office, but added that he would first see another Comedy. Mr. *Crown* endeavouring to excuse himself, by telling the King, that he plotted slowly and awkwardly; the King replyed, that he would help him to a Plot, and so put into his Hands the *Spanish* Comedy called *Non pued Esser.* Mr. *Crown* was oblig'd immediately to go to work upon it; but, after he had writ three Acts of it, found to his Surprise, that the *Spanish* Play had some time before been translated, and acted, and damn'd, under the Title of *Tarugo's Wiles, or the Coffee-house.* Yet, supported by the King's Command, he went boldly on and finish'd it . . .[19]

On the last day of rehearsal, according to Dennis, when expectations of the play's fortune were high, and Crowne was anticipating the fulfillment of the king's promise, he met Cave Underhill coming from the playhouse with the word that the king was dead. Actually, Charles II lived for three days after Underhill's alarm, but Crowne's hopes of preferment were lost with the accession of James II. The play nevertheless exceeded all early promise, and was played and reprinted until late in the eighteenth century. It appeared in German as *Sir Phantast, oder Es Kann Nicht Seyn* in 1767, and in an adaptation, *Unmögliche Sache,* in 1782.

By 1689 Crowne again contemplated satire of the Catholic

[19] Dennis, II, 405.

party, this time with stronger personal motives than in the time of the Popish Plot, and with the greater freedom afforded by the reign of William and Mary. The result was *The English Frier,* which contained a satirical portrait of a scheming, lewd, and covetous priest. The stage career of this comedy was violent and presumably brief. On opening night the audience rioted, and the actors could not be heard. Crowne himself explained that the players "thought fit to keep it down, to preserve the peace of the stage, for otherwise they would never have given over a play which brought so much good company together, as this did on the third day, by its own strength".[20]

Although White sees in the play the influences of Molière's *Tartuffe* and *L'Avare,* he concludes that the friar, Father Finical, was intended as a caricature of the Jesuit Edward Petre, clerk of the royal closet to James II, whom James wished to have appointed Archbishop of York. The immorality of the priest in Crowne's play had been charged against Father Petre, who was believed by many to be the father of the young prince born June 10, 1688.

Again utilizing a Spanish source, Crowne produced a blank verse comedy in 1694, entitled *The Married Beau.* This time his original was not a drama, but a *novela* included in Cervantes's *Don Quixote,* "El Curioso Impertinente". Apparently *The Married Beau* brought its author more reward than any play since *Sir Courtly Nice,* yet, as White points out in his study, younger men of greater talent – Congreve, Farquhar, and Vanbrugh – were coming forward, and with them the older dramatist could not compete. With the production of *The Married Beau* "the period of Crowne's prosperity and prominence draws to a close".[21]

Moreover, Crowne's health had begun to fail. In the Epistle to the Reader attached to *Caligula* (1698) he writes, "I have for some few years been disordered with a distemper, which seated itself in my head, threatened me with an epilepsy, and frequently took from me not only all sense but almost all signs of life, and in my intervals I wrote this play".[22] While Queen Mary was alive

[20] Crowne, *Works,* IV, 22-24.
[21] White, p. 46.
[22] Crowne's last recorded work, a comedy called *Justice Busy,* was acted

Crowne received sums of money, but with her death, he began to address frequent, though unsuccessful, petitions to King William for the recovery of his estate. In 1701 he was ridiculed in a satire, *The Town display'd in a Letter*:

> C——n, with a feeble pace and hoary hairs,
> Has just outliv'd his wit by twenty years.[23]

Under Queen Anne he received, upon petition, a grant of £50 annually during his last years. Official treasury papers record grants of money to him as late as November 30, 1706, but after that date no record of his income is to be found. Crowne lived until 1712, when he was buried in the church of St. Giles-in-the-Fields on April 27. The church, which customarily noted the parentage of parishioners buried there, recorded only Crowne's name and burial date, a final proof of the poverty and obscurity in which he ended his life.

C. STAGE HISTORY

Sir Courtly Nice was the first play to come to the stage after the death of Charles II, and following its opening at the Theatre Royal, Drury Lane, on May 4, 1685, it was acted more than ninety times before 1800 in London, at Court, and by groups of strolling players in the provinces. At Court, comedies had been the favorites since 1660; Crowne's new play was to compete in frequency of court performance with Dryden's *Secret Love; or, The Maiden Queen,* Aphra Behn's *The Rover,* and another Spanish play suggested to its adapter by King Charles, Sir Samuel Tuke's *The Adventures of Five Hours.*[24] The first performance of *Sir*

---

at Lincoln's Inn Fields *circa* 1699, but not printed, because in Downes's phrase, it "prov'd not a living Play", though Mrs. Bracegirdle, "by a Potent and Magnetick Charm in Performing a Song in't, caus'd the *Stones of the Streets to fly in the Men's Faces.*" (John Downes, *Roscius Anglicanus,* p. 45.) This cryptic tribute to the actress is explained by R. G. Noyes as a quotation from a song in the play. ("Mrs. Bracegirdle's Acting in John Crowne's *Justice Busy*", *Modern Language Notes,* XLIII (1928), 390-91.)

[23] Quoted by A. H. Bullen in his article on Crowne in the *Dictionary of National Biography,* V, 245.

[24] Eleanore Boswell, *The Restoration Court Stage,* p. 108.

Courtly Nice before James II on November 9, 1685, was followed
by two others in 1686; the play was acted before William and
Mary on April 30, 1690, and before George I on October 6, 1718.
The latter was one of a series of seven performances [25] given at the
newly fitted theatre in Hampton Court under the direction of
Steele, who is supposed to have told Lord Sunderland, the son-in-
law of Marlborough, that the King liked the entertainment "so
terribly well . . . that I was afraid I should have lost all my actors;
for I was not sure the King would not keep them to fill the place
at Court, which he saw them so fit for in the play". Doran states
that George I initiated a new policy in regard to payment of the
players, who, when they acted at Whitehall in earlier times, "cost
but the poor fee of £20", because they played at their own theatre
in the afternoon and before the Court at night. London players at
Hampton Court were given their ordinary wages and their travel-
ing expenses, and were to be ready to act there at a day's notice.
The Lord Chamberlain "found the wax-lights, and furnished the
'household music', while the players' wardrobe and 'traps' generally were conveyed from old Drury down to Hampton in a *'Chaise
Marine'* at his Majesty's expense". The cost of the seven plays
that included *Sir Courtly Nice* was £350, to which King George
generously added "a couple of hundred more, as a guerdon to the
managers, who had professed that the honor of toiling to afford
his Majesty pleasure was sufficient recompense in itself"! [26]

The long career of *Sir Courtly Nice* in the provinces began at
Bath in 1703, with Colley Cibber in the title part and Anne Oldfield as Leonora. Two performances at William Pinkethman's
theatre in Greenwich, June 28 and September 7, 1710, are
recorded, as is a performance at Oxford in the summer of 1713.
On February 25, 1717, there was a performance by the Duke of
Norfolk's Company at "the White-Horse at Troas" (Trowse) just
outside the city of Norwich. The London Company acted *Sir
Courtly* in Canterbury during the summer of 1739 and again in
1741, at which time it was billed as being "esteem'd a Masterpiece

[25] The other plays were *Hamlet, The Constant Couple, Love for Money,
Volpone,* and *Rule a Wife and Have a Wife.*
[26] John Doran, *Annals of the English Stage,* II, 132-34.

of Dramatick Poetry for the Opposition of Characters it contains,
by King Charles the Second, by whose Command and Assistance
it was wrote". On the same program, as an after-piece, was
Carey's *The Dragon of Wantley,* which had been played "sixty
odd nights successively at Covent Garden".[27] In 1746 *Sir Courtly*
was presented at Thomas Chapman's theatre at Richmond Hill,
and in 1747 at Ipswich, by the Norwich Company.[28]

In London *Sir Courtly Nice* continued to be played at Drury
Lane for over half a century, although after 1758 it was most often
seen at Covent Garden. The change of taste that accompanied
the Age of Sensibility apparently did not seriously diminish the
popularity of Crowne's comedy, as it did that of some other
Restoration plays. King Charles, when the unfinished play was
brought to him, is supposed to have deplored the absence of
"smut";[29] Mrs. Behn two years later appealed her own conviction
of licentiousness by reference to the greater indecency of Crowne's
play.[30] In 1701 the actors were brought before the grand jury for
Middlesex for uttering offensive speeches in the play,[31] but Dennis
could write in 1719:

All that is of *English* Growth in *Sir Courtly Nice* is admirable; for
tho' we find in it neither the fine Designing of *Ben. Johnson;* nor the
general and masculine Satyr of *Wycherly,* nor that Grace, that Delicacy, nor that Courtly Air which make the Charms of *Etherege;* yet
is the Dialogue so lively and so spirited . . . four . . . Characters are so
entirely new, yet general and so important, are drawn so truly . . .
that tho' I have more than twenty times read over this charming
Comedy, yet I have read it, not only with Delight but Rapture. And
'tis my Opinion, that the greatest Comick Poet that ever liv'd in any
Age, might have been proud to have been the Author of it.[32]

The comic role of Sir Courtly was created by William Mountfort

[27] Sybil Rosenfeld, *Strolling Players and Drama in the Provinces (1660-
1765),* pp. 235-36.
[28] Rosenfeld, p. 103.
[29] The anecdote, from Oldmixon's *History of England* (1730), is quoted
in Montague Summers's *Restoration Comedies,* pp. xli-xlii.
[30] See the preface to the printed text of *The Lucky Chance* (1687), as
quoted in M. Summers, *The Restoration Theatre,* pp. 189-90.
[31] R. G. Noyes, *Ben Jonson on the English Stage (1660-1776),* pp. 54-55.
See Explanatory Notes.
[32] Dennis, II, 406.

and taken over by Colley Cibber and his rival George Powell after Mountfort's death in 1692. Mountfort, who had played Sparkish in Wycherley's *Country Wife,* was still better as the fop in Crowne's play, according to Cibber, who praised "the insipid, soft civility, the elegant and formal mien, the drawling delicacy of voice, the stately flatness of his address, and the empty eminence of his attitudes". Mountfort had a pleasant singing voice, which in Cibber's words "set off the last scene of Sir Courtly with an uncommon happiness".[33] Cibber himself played Sir Courtly for over thirty years,[34] Powell having died in 1714. Cibber had little respect for Powell's acting ability, and openly reproved his irregular habits and neglect of roles, but Cibber's own failings are amusingly revealed in Davies's description of him, hastening from the gaming tables to the theatre:

After many an unlucky run at Tom's Coffee-house (in Russell Street), he has arrived at the playhouse in great tranquillity; and then, humming over an opera-tune, he has walked on the stage not well prepared . . . . I have seen him at fault . . . in parts which he had acted a hundred times, and particularly in *Sir Courtly Nice*; but Colley dexterously supplied the deficiency of his memory by prolonging his ceremonious bow to the lady, and drawling out 'Your humble servant, madam', to an extraordinary length; then taking a pinch of snuff, and strutting deliberately across the stage, he has gravely asked the prompter, what is next? [35]

In the provinces, the leading actor of the Norwich Company, Joseph Peterson, took the role of Sir Courtly in the forties, and Henry Woodward and Samuel Foote played the part at Drury Lane, Foote in 1746 and 1753, and Woodward in 1751, 1764, and 1770.

The "gracioso" character, Crack, was originally played by Anthony Leigh, a comic whose other roles at about this time

[33] Colley Cibber, *Apology,* ed. R. W. Lowe, pp. 188-89.
[34] Cf. Lowe, *Apology,* pp. 267-69: "During the season of [1734-35 Cibber] acted Lord Foppington, Sir John Brute, Sir Courtly Nice, and Sir Fopling Flutter . . . . In the season 1735-36 he acted Sir Courtly Nice and Bayes." These performances do not appear in the Avery-Scouten list, which gives 1729 as Cibber's last appearance in Crowne's play.
[35] Davies, *Dramatic Miscellanies,* III, 480, as quoted by Lowe, *Apology,* p. 302 *n.*

included Scaramouch in Aphra Behn's *Emperor of the Moon*
(1687), the French barber La Roch in Shadwell's *Bury Fair*
(1689), and Sir William Belfond, the outwitted father in Shadwell's *The Squire of Alsatia* (1688), the latter a performance
superlatively praised by Cibber for "spirited Variety". After
Leigh's death in 1692, the role of Crack was taken by Richard
Estcourt, who was highly commended by Steele, but dismissed
by Cibber as a mimic. William Pinkethman, who played the part
twelve times between 1708 and 1722, was the best of Tony
Leigh's immediate successors. Cibber says that he was particularly
well adapted to such farcical roles as that of Crack because he
"delighted more in the whimsical than the natural". That he was
the hero of the footmen in the upper gallery, whose tastes ran to
slapstick, may be seen from the following couplet in the prologue
to Cibber's *Love Makes a Man* (1700):

> To please all tastes, we'll do the best we can;
> For the galleries, we've Dicky and Will. Penkethman.

Pinkethman exploited his low-comedy appeal to the masses by
playing at fairs, and eventually had his own successful theatres in
Greenwich and Richmond. Leo Hughes believes that the following
paragraph, reprinted by Sybil Rosenfeld from *Heraclitus Ridens,*
24-28 August, 1703, describes Pinkethman's desertion from his
troupe to play more profitably at Bartholomew Fair:

Deserted from her Majesty's company of stage players at Bath with
all his cloaths and accoutrements after having receiv'd advanc'd
money: a man that writes himself a *famous comedian*: Suppos'd to
have enter'd himself among the socks and buskins in Bartholomew
Fair, and taken his journey through the allurement of a thirty pound
bag. If he will return to his quarters at the Bath in 14 days, he shall
be kindly receiv'd; otherwise his twelve-penny admirers will proceed
against him with the utmost severity.[36]

Josias Miller took over the role of Crack from Pinkethman, and
late in the eighteenth century Ned Shuter played Crack, in 1764
and 1770, before his successes as Hardcastle in Goldsmith's *She*

---

[36] Leo Hughes, *A Century of English Farce*, p. 184. See also Rosenfeld,
p. 169.

Stoops to Conquer, and Sir Anthony Absolute in Sheridan's *The Rivals.*

Surly, Hothead, and Testimony, the "humor" characters of *Sir Courtly Nice,* were originated by Philip Griffin, Cave Underhill, and Thomas Gillow. Of these, Gillow was the least prominent, being an actor of secondary parts, including that of "Melanax, A Spirit" in Dryden and Lee's *The Duke of Guise* (1682), a role which Dryden declared to have been "murder'd in the *Acting*".[37] Griffin was said by Downes to be "unequaled" both in the role of Surly in Crowne's play and in that of Sir Edward Belfond in *The Squire of Alsatia,*[38] but Underhill was more highly regarded by Cibber, who called him "a correct and natural comedian".[39] He was famous for the part of the Gravedigger in *Hamlet,* and for playing rustic and stupid characters, such as Lolpoop, the Yorkshire servant in *The Squire of Alsatia,* and Justice Clodpate in *Epsom Wells.* He outlived his contemporaries Jevon, Nokes, and Leigh, and was still on the stage to play Sir Wilful Witwoud in Congreve's *The Way of the World* in 1700. William Bullock, the successor to several roles of Nokes and Leigh, and the comic partner of Pinkethman, followed Underhill as Hothead from 1706 to the time of his desertion of Drury Lane for Rich's company in 1714. Henry Woodward, the famous eighteenth-century comedian at Drury Lane, whose parts ranged from fops like Brisk of *The Double Dealer* and Sir Fopling Flutter to the erring prentice Quicksilver in *Eastward Ho* and to Bobadill and Sir Andrew Aguecheek, exhibited the same versatility in Crowne's play, acting Hothead between his appearances as Sir Courtly. Henry Norris, "Jubilee Dicky", played Testimony in 1706 and 1710, but the actor best known for the role was the low comedian Benjamin Johnson, who played it sixteen times between 1707 and 1727.

Elizabeth Leigh, who, according to Cibber, "had a good deal of humour, and knew how to infuse it into the affected mothers, aunts, and modest stale maids that had miss'd their market",[40]

---

[37] Downes, *Roscius Anglicanus* (1708), ed. Montague Summers, p. 215.
[38] Downes, as quoted in Summers, *Restoration Comedies,* p. xliv.
[39] Cibber, *Apology,* p. 214.
[40] Cibber, *Apology,* p. 222.

originated the role of the Aunt in *Sir Courtly Nice* and climaxed her career as Lady Wishfort in *The Way of the World*. The part of Belguard, the jealous brother, created by Edward Kynaston, passed to John Mills, who held it from 1706 to 1722, and then to lesser actors. Leonora, the heroine, was first played by Elizabeth Barry, the mistress of Rochester, long popular on the stage in both tragedy and comedy. As a comic actress she was remembered for her portrayal of the jealous Mrs. Loveit in *The Man of Mode* and the neglected wife, Lady Easy, in Cibber's *The Careless Husband,* the performance with which she closed her career in 1710. The role of Leonora was the first stage success for Anne Oldfield, who at sixteen had delighted Farquhar at the Mitre Tavern, where her aunt was hostess, by reading aloud from Beaumont and Fletcher's *The Scornful Lady*. During rehearsal Cibber had "so cold an expectation of her abilities"[41] that he could scarcely bring himself to read through the scenes, but after the performance he shared the enthusiasm of Farquhar and Vanbrugh which had induced Rich to hire the novice actress. During a long and successful career Mrs. Oldfield portrayed Sylvia in *The Recruiting Officer,* Indiana in *The Conscious Lovers,* Lady Betty Modish in *The Careless Husband,* and, although she shared it with others, retained the role of Leonora in Crowne's play until 1729. In 1746 and 1751 Dr. Johnson's favorite comedienne Kitty Clive played Leonora, the last of the well-known actresses to be seen in the role.

D. SOURCES

I

The long-continued popularity of *Sir Courtly Nice* with Restoration and eighteenth-century audiences constitutes only a portion of the play's interest for the student of literary history. In many ways this play is a representative comedy of the period. Although the level of its wit falls below the median for the plays of Etherege and Congreve, and the dialogue lacks the incisive vigor of Wycher-

---

[41] Cibber, *Apology,* p. 368.

ley's best writing, within its structure may be found most of the details of plot and character that comprise the *genre* of Restoration comedy. In other respects it seems to anticipate the early eighteenth-century drama, in its portrayal of the hero as a "true lover"[42] rather than as a rake, and the later novel in its faithfulness to middle-class social portraiture. For the conventional background of titled aristocracy does not carry the conviction of authenticity that it does in Etherege's plays. Crowne's lords and ladies are not genuine. Their arrogance is imitative and overdone and more than a trifle vulgar; it lacks the authority of Dorimant's easy and graceful outrageousness. Compared with the fancies of Sir Fopling Flutter, that "offspring of an orchid and an idiot",[43] the delicacy of Sir Courtly Nice seems labored, and his effeminacy distastefully emphasized. Leonora comes close to being a strumpet, without the comic license of Hoyden or Miss Prue; in comparison with the resources of a Millamant, her upstart deceitfulness is common and contemptible. The most original touches in the play, the righteous indignation of the Tory Hothead, the stolid British embarrassment of Belguard in the scenes with the supposedly imbecile Sir Thomas Callicoe, and the managerial preoccupations of the Aunt, are observations from middle-class life in the manner of Smollett and Fielding. The humour-characterization of Surly, Testimony, and Hothead is well within the tradition of seventeenth-century drama derived from the Jonsonian pattern. The ingenious servant is a stock character, and the Aunt a recurrent type. The comic infatuation of the latter with Sir Courtly is a familiar mockery of the main story line, which, as in all such plays, consists of love-intrigue. The two sets of lovers, Leonora and Farewell, Violante and Belguard, each serving as a foil for the other, are also typical of Restoration comedy plotting. The love-contract or stipulation of conditions before marriage on the part of the women is, as Kathleen Lynch points out in *The Social Mode of Restoration Comedy,* a stock device of *precieuse* literature, one of the most pervasive influences upon the drama of the

---

[42] The phrase is that of John Harrington Smith in *The Gay Couple in Restoration Comedy,* pp. 119-20.
[43] Louis Kronenberger, *The Thread of Laughter,* p. 51.

seventeenth century. The incident is, of course, wrought to comic perfection in Congreve's *The Way of the World*.

Crowne's play is representative also of the comedies known to have been derived, at least in part, from *comedias* of the Spanish Golden Age, of which much has been surmised but little verified by scholars chiefly interested in English literature. The question of the influence of the "Spanish plot" upon the comedies of the Restoration is one which has been debated intermittently since the plays themselves were written. Gerard Langbaine's *Account of the English Dramatick Poets* (1691) is the primary source for later writers who, often without explanation, have added to and subtracted from the list of seventeen plays that he attributed to Spanish plays or prose romances. Langbaine subsequently acquired a reputation for having been an "overingenious compiler of sources",[44] but in actuality his assertions are more easily verified or disproved than those of some modern scholars.

The nineteenth-century critic A. W. Ward, in his *History of English Dramatic Literature,* omitted nine of the titles mentioned by Langbaine, but added others to bring the total of dramas supposedly derived from the Spanish to twenty-five. Although he consulted works by students of the Spanish drama, Ward was often content to attribute a particular play to "some Spanish source". Nevertheless, he did demonstrate his awareness of the complexity of any discussion of literary influences. Although he did not read Spanish, he saw certain obvious differences between the drama of the Golden Age and that of the Restoration, and it was his opinion that "the connexion between the Spanish and the English drama in this period, which is sometimes assumed to have been extremely intimate, will, the more the subject is inquired into, be found to reduce itself to a narrow range of indebtedness on the part of our writers".[45]

In the nineteen-twenties, a number of specialists in the Restoration drama, among them Allardyce Nicoll and Montague Summers, indicated the desirability of further research in the matter

---

[44] W. S. Clark II, ed., *Dramatic Works of Roger Boyle, Earl of Orrery,* I, 373.

[45] A. W. Ward, *History of English Dramatic Literature,* III, 266-67.

of Spanish influence, while the attitude of Ward was maintained by Kathleen Lynch, who stated that the " 'cloak and sword' type of comedy ... proved too decidedly nationalistic in spirit to become fused successfully with, or in any memorable way to change, the current of English comedy of manners".[46] Writing in 1959, John Loftis has revived the issue in a periodical article, contending that "the borrowing from Spanish drama has been underestimated", and that "many Spanish plays appeared on the English stage during the Restoration and eighteenth century". More specifically, he adds:

Among the English writers who took material for plays, either directly or indirectly, from the Spanish dramatists were John Dryden, George Digby Earl of Bristol, Sir Samuel Tuke, William Wycherley, John Crowne, Sir John Vanbrugh, Richard Steele, Susannah Centlivre, Christopher Bullock, Richard Savage, and Robert Dodsley.[47]

The task of searching out sources and analogues in Spanish drama for the plots of Restoration plays is one which can never be satisfactorily accomplished by a scholar working independently. Much work remains to be done by students of Spanish literature in editing plays and establishing accurate bibliographies of individual authors. Greater knowledge of Spanish language and literature is required of scholars in the field of English literary history. Except in isolated cases, such as Allison Gaw's detailed study of Sir Samuel Tuke's adaptation of Coello's *Los empeños de seis horas,* and the briefer articles of Loftis and J. U. Rundle on the relations between Cibber, John Leanerd, and Tirso de Molina, and between Wycherley and Calderón,[48] Restoration versions of Spanish plays and *novelas* have not been compared closely with their originals, and little attempt has been made to analyze the significance of their departure from or adherence to their sources. Nor has a careful study yet been made of the Spanish plays brought to the English stage through adaptations

---

[46] Kathleen Lynch, *The Social Mode of Restoration Comedy,* pp. 121-22.

[47] John Loftis, "Spanish Drama in Neoclassical England", *Comparative Literature,* XI (1959), 30.

[48] Allison Gaw, "Tuke's *Adventures of Five Hours,* in Relation to the 'Spanish Plot' and to John Dryden", *Studies in English Drama,* ed. Gaw; J. U. Rundle, "Wycherley and Calderon", PMLA, LXIV (1949), 701-07.

from the French drama. It has been almost customary for scholars to make no distinction between first-hand and second-hand borrowings and to ignore the French version of a play ultimately derived from the Spanish. Finally, no attempt has been made to study the dramas of the Spanish *siglo de oro* and the English Restoration as common products of a most challenging cultural epoch – the Late Renaissance.

Agustín Moreto, from whose comedy *No puede ser guardar una mujer Sir Courtly Nice* was adapted, was a courtier and a dramatist of polish and precision, if not of great originality. Indeed, *No puede ser* itself represents a re-working of the plot of Lope de Vega's *El mayor imposible.* Gerald Brenan describes Moreto in *The Literature of the Spanish People* as "the playwright of a refined and self-contained court, cut off from the general life of the country and given up, on the surface at least, to a life of love affairs and pleasure".[49] His relative position with regard to Lope de Vega and to Calderón is roughly comparable to Crowne's rank in the company of Etherege and Congreve, although no comparison may be drawn between the latter writers and the greatest of the Spanish dramatists. Moreto is best known for *El desdén con el desdén,* a play in which a princess who believes she is incapable of love is won by a man who pretends not to love her, and for *El lindo Don Diego,* the title character of which is a vain and preposterous fop. *No puede ser,* though perhaps not a masterpiece, is a lively and witty combination of "thesis play" and intrigue comedy. It pictures a way of life that is aristocratic almost in the Platonic sense. Its characters are, with the exception of the obstinate Don Pedro, highly intelligent, and the women are, like Shakespearean heroines, independent without vulgarity. Tarugo, an ancestor of Figaro, is a worthy representative of the *gracioso,* and Manuela typical in her down-to-earth echoes of her mistress's refined sentiments. That the Restoration should have found Moreto's comedy excessively proper is not surprising, but certainly the play is maligned by historians of English drama, among them Arthur F. White, who suggest that it wanted "improving" at the

---

[49] Gerald Brenan, *The Literature of the Spanish People,* p. 314.

hands of a dramatist such as John Crowne. *No puede ser* is a deservedly well-known comedy, in its own way representative of its period. For a discussion of influences and parallel techniques in the drama of both countries, the relationship between the Spanish play and its English counterpart presents an interesting point of departure.

Since *comedia* is a more inclusive term in Spanish than *comedy* in English, it is convenient to compare with Restoration comedy only *comedias de capa y espada,* that is, cape-and-sword or intrigue comedies, comedies of the *figurón* or humour-character, and a group of plays categorized by writers on the Spanish drama in various ways, that fit the English definition of comedy of manners. The foregoing represent only a fraction of the plays written for the Spanish theatre of the seventeenth century. Religious plays, historical dramas, plays of peasant life and of the supernatural, which must be disregarded here because they have no parallels in the Restoration period in England, combine to make the Spanish drama extremely rich in theme and idea, and therefore perhaps more worthy of comparison with the Elizabethan period in English literature than with the more limited period of the Restoration.

The play of cape-and-sword is, as the name suggests, a romantic adventure plot, the personages of which belong to the upper social classes. It is derived principally from the Italian *commedia dell'arte,* and its producton was directly influenced by the latter, since Italian companies presented plays in Spain during the sixteenth century. Hugo Rennert, in his study of the Spanish stage, observes that "the name of the male lover in these *commedie,* Fulvio, Valerio, Ottavio, Leandro ... and of the female lover, *la comica accesa,* Isabella, Lucinda, Leonora ... we find very frequently in the comedies of Lope". There is also much similarity in the situations:

They recur from piece to piece with inconsiderable changes, each with the same mistakes, the same quarrels, the same night scenes, where one person is taken for another in the darkness; the same misunderstandings – *scene equivoche,* etc.[50]

[50] Hugo Rennert, *The Spanish Stage in the Time of Lope de Vega,* pp. 44-45.

The comedies of manners utilize some of the stock situations of
the romantic intrigue, but attempt greater accuracy in portraying
the customs of contemporary society. Here, as in the intrigue
plays, "honor" is exhaustively debated, and the problems of love
treated from many points of view. Some of these plays reveal the
desire for release from the social restraint of the feudal hierarchy,
and for greater personal freedom, particularly on the part of
women. Perhaps there was some breakdown of the social pattern;
Kathleen Gouldson, in an essay on the portrayal of social conditions in the comedies of Francisco de Rojas-Zorrilla, presents a
composite picture that has its parallel in Restoration England:

Since work was to be avoided, there were necessarily many who had
to live by their wits and keep up the appearance of wealth, whatever
their actual poverty. In *Abre el ojo* we see several representatives of
the impecunious gentry who were so common. Clara is a social para-
site, and sponges on all her suitors since she has no income of her
own; when she receives gifts she usually sends them to neighbours
and other friends in the hope of drawing a bigger gift in return. Don
Clemente . . . is reduced to selling his father's silver salt-cellar. Don
Juan . . . asks his landlady not to demand rent while he is away from
his rooms . . . he has bored a hole through to the next compartment, so
that he may read by his neighbour's light . . . . Laín, the old servant
in *La Hermosura y la desdicha,* says that if he becomes rich he will
not be the first to rise in the world . . . one who now lives as a grand
lady under the name of Doña Laurencia was formerly the scullery-
maid Lorenza.[51]

The comedy of the *figurón* is an intellectualized comedy of
manners. In this type of play, for which the dramatist Juan Ruiz
de Alarcón is principally remembered, a "humour", such as un-
truthfulness, ingratitude, or malicious gossip, characterizes the
protagonist and largely directs the action, although mistaken identity and other devices of the intrigue plot may be employed to
support the main theme, which, as in Jonson and his successors,
is the curing of the humour and the re-establishment of balance
and common sense. The background of such a play is usually
contemporary Madrid, and the manners depicted are, as with

---

[51] Kathleen Gouldson, "Three Studies in Golden Age Drama", *Spanish
Golden Age Poetry and Drama,* ed. Allison Peers, p. 114.

Jonson, exaggerations of follies to be observed there and then, but, in another sense, everywhere and always. Satire is most direct in these plays, but the note of cynicism, by no means absent from Spanish literature of the period, is remarkably less prevalent in the *comedia* than in the Restoration drama. Doubtless the firm control of the Church is responsible for the greater stability of Spanish society and the consequent moderation of caricature, satire, and plainness of speech – the comic correctives – in the theatre.

Critical study of *Sir Courtly Nice* did not appear in print until 1922. In that year an edition of the play by Montague Summers was published in his *Restoration Comedies,* a monograph upon the career of Crowne by Arthur F. White was issued by Western Reserve University, and a bibliography of Crowne's works by George Parker Winship was printed at Harvard. Summers's edition, apparently derived from the 1703 quarto of the play, is an inaccurate text, and the prefatory material is scanty. White's monograph presents plot summaries of both *Sir Courtly Nice* and its original, Moreto's *No puede ser,* together with a brief commentary concerning Crowne's technique of adaptation. White also includes an account of Thomas St. Serfe's version of *No puede ser, Tarugo's Wiles; or, The Coffee-house,* which was acted in 1667 without success, and of which Crowne was apparently ignorant when he began his own version of the Spanish play.

The frame of Moreto's drama is the meeting of an *academia,* a society devoted to literature, and to brilliant conversation, at the home of Doña Ana Pacheco, at which an argument develops between two young noblemen, Don Felix and Don Pedro, concerning the possibility of preserving a woman's honor. Don Pedro is convinced that it is possible to protect a woman by keeping her in seclusion, and undertakes to prove it by "guarding" his sister, Doña Ines, from all temptation. Don Felix is of the nobler conviction that a woman's honor must be in her own keeping, and determines to show Don Pedro his own folly by courting Doña Ines secretly. With the connivance of Doña Ana and the inspired strategy of his ingenious servant, Tarugo, Don Felix gains access to Don Pedro's house and helps Doña Ines to escape a marriage

of convenience to a man of her brother's choice. Doña Ana, who
loves Don Pedro, but wishes to change his views about the frailty
of women, is rewarded when he admits the fallacy of his theory
and marries her upon more liberal terms of behavior.[52]

Crowne, in his adaptation, abandoned Moreto's device of the
formal debate upon love and honor, a technique reminiscent of
the *précieuse* influence described at length by Miss Lynch in *The
Social Mode of Restoration Comedy*. He ignored also the familiar

---

[52] The central situation of Moreto's play is but slightly altered from that
of Lope de Vega's *El mayor imposible*. In the latter, the queen, who suf-
fers from a consuming melancholy, is diverted by an *academia* attended
by her courtiers. As might be expected, Lope utilizes more fully than does
Moreto the opportunity offered for a display of poetic virtuosity. Opening
the first scene with a prologue in *redondillas,* he shifts to the *romance* for
a song by the court musicians. A Petrarchan sonnet, exaggerated in its
conceptismo, is the first work presented by a member of the *academia.*
Then an enigma is submitted, a kind of emblem-verse, the central metaphor
of which is a heart with an arrow in fetters, a padlock with a key. A
quintilla follows on the subject of love's deceits, and next three *décimas*
"to an ungrateful lady" are delivered by Roberto, the prototype of Don
Pedro, the jealous brother, who first uses the phrase that gives the play its
title, "el mayor imposible." The greatest impossibility, he contends, is that
woman's beauty should cease to be. This gallantry is immediately challenged by the others, who argue that the greatest impossibility is that a
man should prosper under an evil star, that a self-made man should fail
to hate those who knew him in early life, that a fool should become a wise
man, that love should do what money cannot, and finally, that a woman
should be guarded from affronts to her honor. Lisardo (Don Felix of
Moreto's play) then reads a sonnet in which he says that to preserve a
woman's honor when she herself is careless of it is "el mayor imposible".
Lope's play serves as Moreto's model for all the main characters and
for many devices of plot. The melancholy queen schemes, as Doña Ana
does, to embarrass the jealous Roberto (Don Pedro). Lisardo (Don Felix)
sends his valet Ramón (Tarugo) to Diana (Doña Ines) disguised as a
Flemish jewel merchant, and the lover's picture is secretly offered, as in
the plays of Moreto and Crowne. The lover is hidden in the house of the
jealously guarded girl, and assists her escape from her foolish guardian
Fulgencio (Alberto).
Moreto compensates for the loss of poetry with greater dramatic econo-
my in his adaptation of Lope's plot and characters. Because the argument
concerning honor, which implements the intrigue, emerges from the elabo-
rate riddle propounded by Doña Ana, the *academia* scene may be short-
ened and recitation partially replaced with dialogue. By making Doña Ana,
the instigator of the intrigue, also the beloved of its victim, Don Pedro,
Moreto establishes greater tension within the plot and emphasizes the irony
of its resolution.

motif of the wager as a plot situation, and provided a feud between the families of Farewell and Belguard to serve as motivation for Belguard's jealousy of his sister and his enmity toward her lover. The characters of the original play Crowne adapted recognizably, although White overstates when he contends that the role of Tarugo, the *gracioso* of *No puede ser,* is "transferred in its entirety in the role of Crack".[53] Don Pedro of the Spanish play becomes Lord Belguard, Doña Ines becomes his sister Leonora, and Doña Ana, her friend, the scheming Violante. Don Felix appears in the English play as Leonora's lover, Farewell. As White points out,

Don Diego, the shadowy potential rival of Don Felix in *No Puede Ser,* is metamorphosed into the distinctly individualized Sir Courtly Nice. In this case Crowne borrowed only the occasion for his character's existence. In a similar way the role of Alberto, the trusty relative of Don Pedro, whose duty it is to guard the portals of the fortress, is enlarged to include that interesting group of Lord Bellguard's kinsfolk, the amorous aunt, Hothead, and Testimony. For Surly there is no suggestion in the Spanish play. He is Crowne's creation to serve as a dramatic contrast to Sir Courtly.[54]

The total effect of the character and plot alterations in Crowne is to contribute farcical and satirical effects at the expense of the wit of the Spanish original. Although much is added, much is lost. Don Felix in the Spanish play is a thoughtful young aristocrat who engages in a love plot primarily because his views on the subject of love and women's honor have been challenged by a somewhat obtuse and impolite rival in debate. For a time, vindication of his idea is a more important object than the winning of the lady. In the first scene of the comedy he engages in an entertaining argument with his servant Tarugo concerning poets and learned men, occasioned by his mention of the forthcoming *academia* at the home of Doña Ana. When he informs Tarugo that Doña Ana is intellectual as well as beautiful and rich, the *gracioso* replies that this is impossible. His reasoning, supported by popular proverbs and similitudes, is that poetry and learning are incompatible with worldly wealth. Poetry, he says, is a flower in the garden, good to look at, but not to eat.

[53] White, p. 142.
[54] White, p. 142.

> Y él que un jardín entra a ver
> Más presto se irá a buscar
> Espárragos que cenar
> Que las flores para oler.

Shifting his ground somewhat, Tarugo adds that fortune parcels out the good things of life so that no one may have them all. No one would covet another's piece of meat if he knew the size of the bone inside; to the runt of the litter is given the biggest acorn; and finally, poetry is not written by the light of silver candlesticks:

> Sola la poesía es buena
> Hecha a moço de candil.

Don Felix responds with a formal "catalogue" of successful poets and sages, from Homer (who was "muy rico") and Vergil to Petrarch and Ronsard, Guarini and Tasso, Garcilaso and Góngora. A display of wit and ingenious argument is also a feature of the *academia* scene. Each of the guests reads an original poem, and Doña Ana propounds a riddle about an underground fire:

> Este fuego que arde en mí
> Otro fuego le encendió,
> Que arde también como yo,
> Y a un tiempo ardemos así.
> El humo que exhala el fuego
> Conviene a mi perfección;
> Y el cubrirme es por razón
> De que no le exhale luego.
> Mientras que no me consumo,
> Cuando más tierra me das
> Más me abrigas y ardo más,
> Con que he de arrojar más humo.
> No dejando yo de arder,
> Salir en vapor presumo.
> Decid quién soy yo y el humo,
> Que guardar no puede ser.

Don Felix guesses the answer; the hidden fire is a woman in love, and the smoke, the "humo denso", is her honor. The more the fire is banked, the hotter it burns; as smoke must have an outlet, so must there be freedom before there can be honor. Honor, like smoke, "no puede ser guardar".

From the subsequent discussion of this bold idea arises the argument that ends in Don Pedro's vowing to keep his sister under guard. Doña Ines, indignant at this unmerited insult to her integrity, repeats in a speech to her maid, Manuela, the metaphor of the subterranean fire, originally introduced by Doña Ana. A stifled blaze, she says, will produce an explosion. With this view Manuela has much sympathy; last year, during Lent, she fasted of her own volition upon bread and water, but this year, having been ordered to fast,

> Maldito el día que he dejado
> De almorzar y merendar.

Crowne's omission of the philosophical discussions and the scenes from the *academia* weakens the characters of Leonora, Violante, Belguard, Farewell, and Crack – in short, all of the chief figures of the original play. The jealous Don Pedro is foolish and irrational, but Belguard has not even the excuse of rashness in argument to soften the coarseness of his behavior in marrying his sister to a rich fool. Doña Ana, wise and urbane, is amply motivated to intrigue by the mortifying smugness of her future husband, but Violante, in her plotting against Belguard, is bargaining for a questionable form of "liberty" after marriage. Leonora has, of course, every reason to foil her brother's plans for her future, and she provides the ideal comeuppance for the egregious Sir Courtly, but her brazen lies and impudent rejoinders, amusing enough in a low-comic way, are more befitting the kitchen than the drawing-room. There could be no greater contrast to the high-comedy dialogue and the dignified moral plane of Moreto's play.

White observes that Crowne's retention of the principal incidents of *No puede ser* follows from the decision to preserve the role of Tarugo. From another point of view, the retention of the intrigue without its original justification in the debate and the wager distinctly lowers the moral status of Tarugo and his master. It is true that there are explicit references to Tarugo's role of "Celestina"; with disarming frankness he admits to Doña Ines that he is Don Felix's go-between, but in the Spanish play there is none of the cynical bravado and none of the indecency in Crack's admission:

I had an ambition to be of some honourable profession; such as People of Quality undertake. As for instance, Pimping. A Pimp is as much above a Doctor, as a Cook is above a Scullion; when a Pimp has foul'd a Dish, a Doctor scours it.

For Tarugo's homespun with Crowne substituted Crack's more vulgar but more direct form of verbal humor – suggestive *double entendre,* and gibberish and wild exaggeration in his impersonation of "mad" Sir Thomas Callicoe.

Having weakened the main plot which he had chosen to adopt, and with it the characters which it supported, Crowne was forced to create other characters to sustain interest and to provide the chief comic effects. His most important creation, Sir Courtly Nice, in the role of the rival lover, became one of the Restoration trio of famous fops, along with Sir Fopling Flutter and Lord Foppington. As a foil for Sir Courtly's extravagances of delicacy, Crowne provided the slovenly boor, Surly, and for low comedy in the "guarding" of Leonora, the political rivals Testimony and Hothead. The latter is a humour figure, as his name implies; he is easily persuaded to quarrel, but his religious orthodoxy is not satirized. Testimony, who receives the most satirical treatment, is a hypocritical non-conformist in the tradition of Zeal-of-the-land Busy, and in his "licorish tooth" also suggests Fondlewife and Alderman Gripe.

A tradition which extended at least as far back as Lady Loveall in *The Parson's Wedding,* and which was developed in Etherege's Lady Cockwood and Wycherley's Lady Flippant, was available to Crowne in the portrayal of the love-sick spinster Aunt in *Sir Courtly Nice.* Nevertheless, White argues convincingly that Crowne's debt here is to Molière:

The influence of Molière which was so evident in *The Countrey Wit* is not entirely wanting in *Sir Courtly Nice.* The character of the amorous aunt was suggested by Belise in *Les Femmes Savantes.* Sir Courtly, like Clitandre, appeals to the aunt for assistance, and Leonora's aunt, like Belise, mistakes the appeal for a declaration of love. In both incidents the effect is produced by ambiguity of phrase.[55]

The farcical episodes involving the Aunt's passion for Sir Courtly and the latter's discomfiture at having won her instead of Leonora are the high moments of Crowne's play, and detract somewhat from the importance of Crack's stratagems, which are more effective in the original because there are fewer characters and incidents. Crowne does, however, imitate this part of the action closely. In both plays, the *gracioso* gets into the house of the lady as a guest, by disguising himself. In Moreto, he is an *indiano*, or colonist returned with riches from the New World. In Crowne, he is Sir Thomas Callicoe, the son of a wealthy Far Eastern merchant, who brings to the play a pseudo-oriental savor at a date when popular interest in "Bantam" natives had been aroused by the visit of oriental potentates to London. In both plays the servant in disguise pretends eccentricity – Crowne's in an extreme degree – and from his supposed phobias arise the means of preventing discovery. Both are victims of love charms that make them fear to see women, and both develop fits at opportune moments to help their masters escape detection by the jealous brothers. Both have an imaginary marriageable sister, and so may communicate with eligible suitors (Don Felix and Farewell) inside the house. The final trick in each case is to mask or disguise the heroine as a streetwalker to enable her to escape from the house.

Of the many plays studied for parallels in Spanish plots, Crowne's play is unique in the manner of its composition. Having been supplied the Spanish play by the king, the dramatist was obliged to follow it with a degree of faithfulness not usual in such circumstances. And yet one could not say, as Loftis does, that the Spanish comedy "appeared on the English stage". The plot borrowings, extensive as they are, have not re-created the original in spirit or in total effect. In the case of other English plays, adapted more casually, perhaps from several sources rather than from one, it is difficult to believe that the relationship to Spanish dramatic tradition would be closer.

---

[55] White, p. 144.

II

Much that is misleading has been said about the qualities of realism and romanticism in the Restoration drama. The plays have been said to be "realistic" in portrayal of character and "romantic" in plot; the assertion has been made often that plots were imported wholesale from the Spanish and French drama, and the implication has been that Jonsonian comedy accounts for the realism and foreign literatures for all that is romantic and improbable in the situations. Although attention was called by Miss Lynch to the discrepancy between Jonson's theory and his practice, the foregoing assumption is still current and presents a problem of definition and clarification. If realism in fiction is to be conceived as the technique of beginning with characters drawn from life and of constructing the action thereafter in accordance with the psychological processes of these characters as envisioned by the writer, romance in imaginative literature may be defined as storytelling that first visualizes a situation or an action and fits to it the characters as they are needed. This is not to say that the latter method allows no opportunity for development of motivation, or for the expression of the author's attitudes and ideas, but it is characterized by lack of concern for logical consistency. Realism in the sense of verisimilitude – astute psychology, description from observation, and even topical satire or social commentary, may be found in a story that is obviously constructed from traditional fable. Romantic literature in the latter sense has greater freedom than the kind of literature developed in the nineteenth and twentieth centuries – realism in the most restricted meaning of the term. Romance fiction may take liberties with motivation that are not allowed by the scientific attitude of the modern realistic school, it may allow a stylized language to take the place of normal human speech, and it may shift from single-dimension to multiple-dimension in depicting human beings. To this kind of literature Restoration comedy belongs, as does the Spanish *comedia* of the Golden Age.

Both the Spanish comedy and the comedy of the English Restoration tend to superimpose upon the heritage of comic themes and plot devices certain situations depicting affairs of contemporary life, and both embody patterns of behavior, standards, and values that reflect, to some degree at least, contemporary social philosophies. Common to both is appreciation of wit, in the broadest interpretation, embracing imagination, acumen, judgment, decorum, and refinement of intellectual taste, in addition to gaiety, sophistication, and verbal facility. Thomas Fujimura in his study *The Restoration Comedy of Wit* develops the thesis that the comedy of the Restoration is more properly comedy of wit than comedy of manners, and observes that the actions of these plays involve not real people or even humours, but "the figures of Truewit, Witwoud, and Witless in a variety of outwitting situations".[56] In examining the intellectual background of wit comedy, Fujimura states that "the key words are naturalism, libertinism, and skepticism".

The Truewits are egoistic and libertine, and they conform to Hobbes' description of young men as "violent in their desires. Prompt to execute their desires. Incontinent. Inconstant, easily forsaking what they desired before. Longing mightily, and soon satisfied". They are also "lovers of mirth, and by consequence such as love to jest at others".[57] This description is truer to the character of Dorimant, Bellmour, Horner, and Courtall than the "manners" description of them as butterflies posturing before the social mirror. These young men are drawn as egoists and libertines, concerned principally with the objects of their desire or aversion: they pursue the pleasures of wine, women, and wit, and they ridicule Witless, Witwoud, and unnatural creatures. It was precisely on these grounds that Dennis defended the character of Dorimant against Steele's moralistic censure: Dorimant is portrayed as malicious, egoistic, and libertine because that is the true nature of young men.[58]

Doubtless the atmosphere of skepticism in Protestant England described above accounts for much of the disparity of moral tone that exists between the drama of that country and the Spanish. It is, however, interesting because of this disparity to note that Miss Gouldson also applies the word "libertine" to behavior of

[56] Thomas Fujimura, *The Restoration Comedy of Wit*, p. 17.
[57] Thomas Hobbes, *The Whole Art of Rhetoric* II, 14, in *The English Works*, VI, 466-67. Quoted in Fujimura, pp. 49-50.
[58] Fujimura, p. 50.

the upper middle classes depicted in the plays of Rojas-Zorrilla, pointing out the contempt felt by young people for work and serious purposes, the indulgence in flirtation for the excitement of the game, the wavering of religious conviction, "the empty life of the rich, and the hypocrisy of the would-be rich".[59] Fujimura himself relates the ideal of the Truewit and the Restoration vogue of the "similitude" to non-dramatic works of Spanish literature. These include Baltasar Gracián's *El discreto* (1646), a treatise upon the ideal qualities of the courtier, emphasizing the attributes of perception, taste, and decorum, and the same writer's critical work *Agudeza y arte de ingenio* (1640), which was well known to English writers, among them William Wycherley.

If the chief interest of Restoration comedy lies in its witty repartée and in its ironic projection of contemporary moral and social values, intellectual interest in the *comedia* is centered in ingenuity of plot and in the poetic qualities or rhetorical effects of the dialogue. Something of the Renaissance enthusiasm for the treatise is to be found in Lope de Vega's compendious treatment of problems related to love: the conflict of *buen amor,* "true love", with *loco amor,* or destructive passion; the rival claims of love and honor; the power of love to endow wisdom; the peril of attempting to force or prohibit love unnaturally. Some of the ideas, such as that of *La dama boba,* later employed by Calderón in *De una causa dos efectos,* are from Ovid; others were current in the Italian *novella* and in the *commedia dell'arte.* The method is reminiscent of the medieval love debate, the actions of the characters in a variety of situations representing theoretical applications of the "laws" of love, but although neither the content nor the technique is precisely original, the result, because of the great volume of the dramatist's work, is unique. The plays, taken together, form a kind of encyclopedia of love, to which Lope's contemporaries and successors made frequent reference for suggestions in plotting and characterization.

That the love debate on stage was popular with audiences may be inferred from the frequent occurrence of the *academia* situation, such as that taken by Moreto from Lope's *El mayor*

[59] Gouldson, p. 118.

imposible. Some of the variations of the *academia* in other plays by Lope are discussed in a preface by one of the editors of *El mayor imposible*:

In *Si no vieran las mujeres* there is an argument ... [concerning] the greatest passion. The prince of *Lo que ha de ser* is in prison, but this does not prevent him from passing his time with his friends in academic pursuits. They indulge in music, verses, witty criticisms, a bit of erudition, and in the inevitable fling at *culteranismo.* In *El guante de doña Blanca* the palace is transformed into an academy, with a lady as presiding genius. The courtiers recite three sonnets upon a set subject, and the clown follows with another in burlesque vein. The prince of *El saber puede dañar,* in order to divert a tedious moment, holds an impromptu academy .... The prince propounds such questions as: "What is the most hateful thing?" and "What do men desire most?" ... In *El milagro por los celos* the king and courtiers recite epigrams they have composed on the same subject.[60]

The academic discussions of poetry, such as the one mentioned above as taking place in *Lo que ha de ser,* are often concerned with a dispute over the development of the language that had parallels in other European countries during the late Renaissance. The literary war in Spain was waged between advocates of *culteranismo,* a movement toward refinement of language, stylization of diction, and a Latinized syntax led by the poet Luis de Góngora, and adherents of *conceptismo,* led by Francisco de Quevedo and by Lope himself. The *conceptistas* disapproved of the obscurity of *culto* poetry, and were primarily concerned for the retention of the purity and integrity of the language. They insisted upon the preservation of the Spanish idiom, but they did favor the use of vivid and sometimes over-ingenious conceits, although Lope expressed the principle of decorum and moderation in their use. It is possible to see, as Fujimura does, the relationship between "Gongorism" and the last phase of the Renaissance preoccupation with linguistic invention in the Restoration comedy of wit. The parallel between *conceptismo* and witty similitudes in English comedy, while not a matter of direct influence, nevertheless establishes a point of contact between the tastes of theatre audiences in the two countries.

[60] Lope Felix de Vega Carpio, *El mayor imposible,* ed. John Brooks, *University of Arizona Bulletin* V (October, 1934), 11.

III

When a struggling dramatist begs patronage of Farquhar's Sir
Benjamin Wouldbe in *The Twin Rivals,* the usurping heir calls
his steward and orders that the playwright be given, not the five
guineas he hopes for, but "the Spanish play that lies in the closet
window". In the same fashion Crowne was "helped to a plot" by
King Charles; a few years earlier Wycherley had gone to the
plays of Calderón for help in plotting *Love in a Wood* and *The
Gentleman Dancing Master.* It is no coincidence that Moreto and
Calderón had themselves adapted plays from Lope de Vega, who
had earlier utilized the themes of other writers, native and foreign.
In analyzing the sources of Lope's plays, Rudolph Schevill has
drawn attention to the number of situations based on disguises,
lies, and concealments which were traditional in the medieval
chivalric romances. The bribery of servants, the exchange of
lovers' tokens, the tricks employed to open a conversation with
a woman and the methods of gaining access to her home, the test
of fidelity – all are commonplaces in the earliest fiction, and most
can be re-discovered in the comedies of the Restoration.

The essential contrast to be established between the treatment
of the basic theme of love in the *comedia* and that in the Restoration comedy rests not upon the difference of customs in the
respective societies, great as it may have been, but upon the stricter
dramatic censorship in Spain and the narrower limits of the comic
genre in England. There is, however, a wider range of treatment
in the plays of both countries than might be expected. The greater
freedom of the English stage allows the hero to conduct several
affairs simultaneously on different social and moral planes, as
Dorimant does with Mrs. Loveit, Belinda, and Harriet, and as
Belfond, Junior does in *The Squire of Alsatia* with Mrs. Termagant, Lucia, and Isabella. A concession to morality is nevertheless implied in the fact that the principal affair must conclude
in marriage, however hasty and ill-contrived. That the last-act
marriage scramble is characteristic of both the English and the
Spanish plays is demonstrated by the dénouement of Rojas-
Zorrilla's *Entre bobos anda el juego* and *La hermosura y la des-*

dicha, and by the ridicule directed at the arbitrary pairing of lovers at the play's end in Cervantes's *La Entretenida.*

The "heroic" treatment of love in the Beaufort-Graciana-Colonel Bruce triangle in Etherege's *The Comical Revenge* and in Wycherley's Valentine-Christina action in *Love in a Wood* was later abandoned, and interest concentrated in the "gay couple" until the 1690's saw the encroachment of sentimental and moralizing themes upon the earlier "love duel". In the *comedia* the treatment of love ranged from the ironic in Rojas-Zorrilla's *Abre el ojo* to the improbably romantic in Tirso de Molina's *Don Gil de las calzas verdes,* and even to the tragic, as in Calderón's *El médico de su honra.*

The majority of situations, particularly in the more serious plays, were in some way concerned with the "honor" theme, a particularly Spanish preoccupation that often baffles the reader of English plays, in many of which exaggerated concern for personal honor is satirized as the sign of witless affectation or hypocrisy, exemplified in the characters of Sir James Formal, the Hispanophile in *The Gentleman Dancing Master,* and Lady Cockwood in *She Wou'd if She Cou'd.* The code of the gentleman, distinguishing him from the merchant and peasant classes, was a Renaissance survival of a medieval concept. In Spanish drama, however, it appears in an exaggerated form. Honor in the plays is seen as the symbol of a gentleman's pride and self-respect; its preservation depends less upon his actions than upon his reputation. The honorable man will tolerate no offense against himself or his family, but he does not hesitate to satisfy his own passions. Dishonor thus consists not in committing, but in receiving an injury.

The possibilities of dramatic complication in the love intrigue play were greatly enhanced by the addition of the honor theme, and its use was extended beyond the plays of court and city life. The revenge taken by the peasants in Lope's *Fuenteovejuna* for the brutal lust of the Comendador and by Pedro Crespo in Calderón's *El alcalde de Zalamea* for a similar offense is represented as being demanded by a sense of personal outrage, a "refined" notion scoffed at by the villains, who are gentlemen in name only.

An ingenious variation of the honor motif occurs in Lope's *La moza de cántaro,* in which the avenger of injured honor is a woman whose father has been insulted by her suitor. Since there is no male relative to take up the cause, Doña Maria visits the lover, Don Diego, in prison and kills him. Before dying, Don Diego himself acknowledges the justice of her action, and in the final scene she is pardoned and rewarded with a more suitable husband.

The idea of lessening the offense to one's honor by taking secret revenge, which is totally foreign to the English code that countenanced only dueling, is essential to the action of many plays of the period. In Calderón's *El médico de su honra* Don Gutierre suspects his wife of an affair with the king's brother the Infante Don Enrique, whose rank precludes direct revenge. The wife is innocent in deed, if not entirely so in mind, but Don Gutierre procures a *sangrador* or blood-letter, directs him to bleed his helpless wife, and after the fatal "accident" is left free to take another wife at the play's end. Similarly, an "accidental" collapse of a wall kills Blanca in Rojas-Zorrilla's *Casarse por vengarse,* and Antonio, in the same author's *Sin honra no hay amistad,* is willing to kill his sister, whom he knows to be innocent, because the suspicions of others demand that he should.

The Spanish dramatist whose plot construction notably differs from that of other dramatists of the Golden Age is Alarcón. In his humour comedy he presents a radically different concept of honor as ethical behavior, and constructs his action by allowing the *figurón* to experience the logical results of his own moral shortcomings. Thus Don Mendo in *Las paredes oyen* loses Doña Ana because his habit of malicious gossip has finally led him into slandering her within her hearing. The main character of *La verdad sospechosa,* a young man who cannot tell the truth, is punished for lying about his love affairs by being forced to marry the woman he said he loved rather than the one he actually wanted for his wife. In both plays the slanders and lies themselves provide ample complications for the action.

Generalizations concerning characterization in the Spanish intrigue play and the Restoration comedy emerge in part from those that may be made concerning the actions of the plays. Thus Fujimura, in applying the formula of interaction between Truewit, Witwoud, and Witless, declares wit to be the basis of Restoration comic characterization. Dobrée, Palmer, Perry, and Miss Lynch, whom Fujimura calls "manners" critics because they evaded the moral strictures of nineteenth-century criticism by assuming that Restoration comedy was manners comedy, describe the comic characters as realistic social portraits. There is evidence to support both views, but a third generalization concerning character portrayal may be drawn from observations of structure in the comedies. Dependence upon the clichés of the romantic adventure plot has imposed in these plays severe limitations upon freedom of characterization and has contributed to the "typing" of characters, despite the efforts of some dramatists to draw character from life, or to create a one-dimensional world of elegance and verbal brilliance in the theatre. It has led also to psychological and moral incongruities that should warn critics from serious discussion of the plays as consistent representations of existing social conditions. Impersonation, supposed mistaken identity, feigned death and madness that could not be expected to deceive a child are presented as commonplaces in a world of sophistication. The ubiquitous situation of the seduction or illicit affair, unless treated seriously as the Spanish treat it, revives impressions of the sex jests of farce and fabliau which are scarcely consonant with intellectual refinement. Gallants who hide in trunks and cupboards and under tablecloths and who go about disguised as clergymen in order to obtain forbidden access to women are no more "manners portraits" than they are models of the Truewit. They are, in their uniformly desirable physical attributes, descendants of the romantic hero, and in their psychology they are allied to their more remote connections, the clever student of the medieval tales and the heroes of Latin comedy. Like the latter, they are often the objects, as well as the authors, of mirth and ridicule; the ironic spirit of their creators reveals itself sufficiently in the suggestion of caricature which their names – Ranger, Wildair, Horner – imply.

In the Spanish drama the *galán,* typified by Don Felix in *No puede ser,* is the equivalent of the Restoration gallant and even more obviously the heir of the chivalric hero. Generally his manner is unlike the cynical flippancy of the rakes, but there are resemblances too. The following speech of a suitor to his intended fiancée, quoted by Miss Gouldson from Rojas-Zorrilla's *Sin honra no hay amistad,* could have been written for one of Wycherley's heroes:

Mi madre es muy rica, y está tán vieja que se morirá dentro de un año, mes más o menos.[61]

The fact that the young lady was favorably impressed with the foregoing recommendation lessens the psychological distance between the heroine of the *comedia* and her pert and witty Restoration counterpart. The latter, though often given to extreme freedom in manners and speech, is nevertheless preserved in a state of technical moral purity, and the romantic heroine is never completely absent from the English scene. Graciana of *The Comical Revenge,* Christina of *Love in a Wood,* and Fidelia of *The Plain Dealer* are eclipsed by Gatty, Harriet, Angelica, and Millamant, but they are reinforced by the arrival of the sentimental heroines in the wake of Amanda in *Love's Last Shift.* In the Spanish plays, there are many enterprising and resourceful female characters. Those drawn by Lope, representing all classes of society, from the peasant girl Laurencia in *Fuenteovejuna* to Doña Maria in *La moza de cántaro* and the queen in *El mayor imposible,* are freely imitated by other dramatists.

Rudolph Schevill remarks in his study of Lope that "there are no mothers in the *comedia*", and adds that all reasons given in defense of the omission of normal family life from the dramatic scene "but emphasize the fact that we are not dealing so much with a limitation imposed upon a great art by etiquette or current manners as with a silent acquiescence in a literary tradition which goes back through centuries of the life of Rome and the Latin nations".[62] This convention, as Schevill makes clear, is accepted in Renaissance drama all over Europe. Foolish old women, of course, there are in abundance, and the nature of their foolishness perhaps reflects upon the part of their creators a hatred of

---

[61] Gouldson, p. 106.
[62] Schevill, p. 17.

hypocrisy that marks them as "humours" of the age. Whatever its exact derivation, the type is represented not only by the aunt in *Sir Courtly Nice* who deceives herself with hope of love from a young exquisite, but by the designing mother of Lope's *La discreta enamorada,* who "has all the gross traits of a duenna, all the undignified weaknesses of a silly old woman who courts the advances of a young gallant, and participates in rendezvous. . .".[63]

The cast-off mistress, such as Mrs. Loveit and Belinda of *Sir Fopling Flutter,* and Mrs. Termagant of *The Squire of Alsatia,* has, for reasons of propriety, no parallel in the *comedia.* This character, invariably the victim of seduction and often of false promises of marriage and eternal love, is a sacrifice to "morality" of the most cynical kind. In surrendering the gallant to his pro-spective wife she must repent her own lapses from virtue or be exposed to raillery or, as in the case of Shadwell's play, genuine cruelty. Although the natural appetites must not be denied, the typical attitude of the Restoration toward the victim of unwise love is expressed in Harriet's speech to Mrs. Loveit:

Mr. Dorimant has been your God Almighty long enough, 'tis time to think of another – A Nunnery is the more fashionable place for such a retreat, and has been the fatal consequence of many a belle passion.

Among secondary male characters, the *lindo* and the fop are satirical exaggerations of the *galán* and the rake. Both may be punished comically by being married off to servant girls or aban-doned mistresses, as the title character is in Moreto's play *El lindo Don Diego,* and as Tattle and Dapperwit are in *Love for Love* and *Love in a Wood.* The returning nabob, or *indiano,* newly rich and often ludicrously smug, is a source of humor in Spanish plays, and the Frenchified Englishman, fresh from an improving year in Paris, amused the English. The complement of the dandy in the English comedies is the country booby, such as Sir Wilful in *The Way of the World,* who represents the negation of all fashion-able and romantic virtues, but who undertakes a clumsy imitation of them. The farcical treatment of seduction adds to the company of the foregoing varied satirical portraits of elderly gallants, hood-

---

[63] Schevill, p. 18.

winked fathers, cuckolds, and outwitted "keepers", among them Sir Oliver Cockwood and Sir Joslin Jolley of *She Wou'd if She Cou'd,* Sir Sampson Legend and Foresight of *Love for Love,* Sir Paul Plyant of *The Double Dealer,* Pinchwife of *The Country Wife,* and Mr. Limberham of *The Kind Keeper.*

The dependence of the intrigue plot upon the *gracioso* or witty servant, who often acts as a catalytic agent, is common to both the English and Spanish plays, although the Spanish version of the character is the more complex and the more varied. Like the Shakespearean clown, he speaks in epigram and poetic conceit, but in his common-sense practicality he resembles his Restoration counterpart. Both owe their origin to the *servus* of the Latin plays, and to the picaresque tradition, and both serve as confidant to monologues of the principal characters, not without frequent comment in an ironic vein. Tarugo in *No puede ser* is a typical example, and in English comedy a close parallel is the intellectually superior Jeremy of *Love for Love,* whose Cambridge experiences and acquaintance with poets have inspired in him a contempt of scholarship:

Does your Epictetus, or your Seneca here ... teach you how to pay your debts without money? ... Will Plato be bail for you? or Diogenes, because he understands confinement, and lived in a tub, go to prison for you?

The Spanish servant often introduces an additional comic dimension by engaging in an intrigue or love affair that runs parallel to that of the gallant and parodies it as in *El estrella de Sevilla* or in Lope's *El acero de Madrid* and *El ausente en el lugar.* The *gracioso* may invent or facilitate deception, as Ramón does in *El mayor imposible* and as Waitwell does in *The Way of the World.*

The tendency to satire and caricature is much more pronounced in the English drama than in the Spanish. As Fujimura observes, the object of this satire often is the unnatural, the hypocritical, the affected, as depicted in the characters of such types as Lady Cockwood and Lady Wishfort, who violate decorum in the pretension to youth and in unseemly pursuit of young men and then hypocritically deny even so much sexual vanity and appetite as is normal and "natural". The fop is satirized for pretension to wit which he does not possess, and for affectation of manners which violate moderation and common sense. Unnatural behavior is further held up to ridicule in old men who fancy young wives. The English direct their laughter at outsiders to the fashionable life of London, at foreigners, tradesmen, soldiers, and the clergy. The latter are satirized chiefly for insincerity and immorality, for human frailty that contrasts with their claim to guardianship of the souls of laymen. "Trust a churchman!" shouts Sir James Formal to his sister Mrs. Caution, "trust a coward with your honour, a fool with your secret, a gamester with your purse, as soon as a priest with your wife or daughter." But even more often than the clergyman, the countryman is cast for the role of Witless. Country pastimes are viewed with the greatest disdain. "I nauseate walking; tis a country diversion", exclaims Millamant. "What young woman of the town could ever say no to a coach and six", asks hare-brained Hippolita, and immediately adds a condition, "unless it were going into the country?" Sir Oliver Cockwood delivers the opinion that "a man had better be a vagabond in this Town than a Justice of Peace in the Country", and Harriet wails, "Methinks I hear the hateful noise of Rooks already – Kaw, Kaw, Kaw – There's musick in the worst Cry in *London*! *My Dill and Cowcumbers to pickle*!"

In direct contrast to the foregoing is the Spanish custom of romanticizing rural life and idealizing the peasantry. The creation of such characters as Juan Labrador, who in Schevill's phrase, "embody the uncorrupted ancient Spanish virtues", emphasizes the contrast between the simple life and the artificial manners of the court. The recognition of personal worth in the countryman Pedro Crespo and his family, and the exposure of the supposed gentlemen who dishonor them is forceful, if implicit, censure of a corrupt social code. Social satire of a restrained order is also unmistakable in Rojas-Zorrilla and in Alarcón. In the works of the latter the "humour" is purged; in those of the former, the aimlessness of contemporary life, the debased manners and sense of honor are often treated ironically.

From the foregoing comparisons it may be seen that fundamental differences in intellectual background, manners, and customs in England and Spain precluded the representation of a Spanish play on the English stage of the Restoration period. The same comparisons nevertheless support the long-standing opinion that many similarities are to be observed between the comedies of the two countries. The transmission of the melodramatic type of action to the theatre in England resulted in a separation of *genres* in accordance with dramatic patterns already accepted in that country, and a consequent heightening of effect in both comic and serious plays. As in the case of *No puede ser,* high comedy was often reduced to farce by being enlivened with native humor tending to caricature and with additional complication of plot. This practice produced analogues such as *Sir Courtly Nice,* true to the outline but not to the spirit of their originals. Such analogues, if studied for evidences of parallel trends and common sources rather than for direct influence and similarity of isolated detail, acquire new significance as documents in the history of European Renaissance drama.

II. TEXT OF THE PLAY

Sir Courtly Nice:

or,

It cannot Be.

A

COMEDY

As it is Acted by His Majesties
Servants.

Written by Mr. Crown.

LONDON,

Printed by *H.H*. Jun. for *R. Bently,* in *Russel-street,*
Covent-Garden, and *Jos. Hindmarsh,* at the
Golden-Ball over against the *Royal Ex-*
change in *Cornhill.* M.DC.LXXXV.

A

THE NAMES OF THE PERSONS

Lord *Belguard*	*Leonora's* Brother, in love with *Violante*.
Sir *Courtly Nice*	A Fop, overcurious in his Diet and Dress: In love with *Leonora*.
Farewel	A young Man of Quality and Fortune, his Rival.
Surly	A morose, ill natur'd, negligent Fellow, in love with *Violante*.
Crack	A young subtle intriguing Fellow.
Hothead	A cholerick Zealot against Fanaticks.
Testimony	A Canting Hypocritical Fanatick.
Violante	A Lady of Quality and Fortune, in love with *Belguard*.
Leonora	*Belguard's* Sister, in love with *Farewel*.
Aunt	*Leonora's* Governess – an old Amorous, envyous Maid.

Scene Covent Garden.

[The Epistle Dedicatory.]

To his Grace the Duke of ORMOND, *Lord* A2
Steward of His Majesties Houshold, Chan-
cellor of the University of Oxford, *Knight*
of the Most Noble Order of the Garter, &c.

May it please your Grace,

This Comedy was Written by the Sacred Command of our
late most Excellent King, of ever blessed and beloved Memory. I had the great good Fortune to please Him often at His
Court in my Masque, on the Stage in Tragedies and Comedies, and so to advance my self in His good opinion; an 10
Honour may render a wiser Man than I vain; for I believe
he had more equals in extent of Dominions than of Understanding. The greatest pleasure he had from the Stage was in
Comedy, and he often Commanded me to Write it, and lately
gave me a *Spanish* Play called *No Puedeser*: *Or, It Cannot
Be.* out of which I took part o' the Name, and design o' this.
I received the Employment as a great Honour, because it
was difficult; requiring no ordinary skill and pains to build
a little Shallop, fit only for the *Spanish* South Seas, into
an *English* Ship Royal; but I believe my self able for 20
the Work, because he thought so, who understood me and
all Men, better than I only knew my self, encourag'd
by a Royal judgment that never was mistaken, I have attained a success I never should have met with, had I only followed my own feeble Genius, which often deceives me.
That I may enjoy the little fortune I have got with the
better reputation, and not ramble the World like a bold out-
law, observing none but my self, I make this humble Ap-

1 Penn 1 has: *To his Grace the Duke of* ORMOND,/ *Lord Steward of
His Majesties Houshold,*/ *Chancellor of the University of* Oxford.
9 Stage in] USC 1, etc.   Stage of Penn 1
20 believe] 1, 2   believed 3
23 by a Royal] USC 1, etc.   by Royal Penn 1
27 ramble] 1, 2   ramble in 3
27 like a bold outlaw] USC, 1, etc.   like a blind Author Penn 1

plication to your Grace. I am sure all the World will approve
my choice. I cannot be guilty of Flattery if I would; nor 30
slander Wit (if I had any) by fulsome and wanton Paintings.
Here will be no Tryal of skill how I can praise, Nature
has done it to my Hands, and devis'd and expos'd finer
Ideas, than I am able to Translate. A gracefulness of Person,
excellence of Understanding, largeness of Heart, a Loyalty,
Gallantry, Integrity, Humility, and many Qualities above
my description. Fortune also has been more wise than usual,
She frequently honours and enriches others to her own disgrace – but here She shares in the Praise, and Commends her
own Wisdome, in what She bestows on your Grace. She has 40
advanc'd Honour in Advancing you, Titles, Greatness and
Command may be prowd, they have attained you. Wealth
has a value in your Hands. 'Tis no vile pardon, poor flatterer,
servile Lacquey, wretched Prisoner; but excellent Minister
of a just wise and liberal Prince. Shou'd I mention all the
Qualities, that have long gained you the highest Honours
from Prince and People, I should rather seem to describe
a Province then a Man; for what single Province can afford
what are at once in your Grace, a General, a Statesman,
a Courtier, and all in perfection; and which is rare in such 50
company, a Martyr. What has your Grace both done and
suffered, for our Religion, Laws, Liberties and Honour? And
not only in the former times of Rebellion, but the latter
of Confusion? When the pretended *Protestants* of the times,
out of their Zeal against all *Popish* Doctrines, abhorr'd you
for adhering to good Works.

As an *English-man,* I am bound in justice, to pay you   A2ᵛ
all the Honours I can. You have been an Ornament, and
support to the Crown and Church of *England,* both in your

42   may be prowd]   USC 1, etc.   may be proved Penn 1 : may
be proud   2, 3
43   Hands.]   2   Hands,   1, 3
48   then a Man]   USC, 1, etc., 2   than a Man   Penn 1, 3
50   a Courtier]   2   Courtier   1, 3
55   abhorr'd]   USC 1, etc., 2, 3   abhorring   Penn 1

Person and Posterity. Many great Men no doubt have sprung 60
from your example, but none equalling those descended
from your self. The late brave Earl of *Ossery,* advanced the
Honour of our Nation, both by Sea and Land. 'Tis hard
to say in which Element he made us most renown'd, and for
which vertue. He was no more to be vanquished by falshood
than fear; Loyalty, Fidelity, and Gallantry, are Vertues
inseparable from the House of *Ormond*; we find 'em in
every branch of it, and at all seasons. The Earl of *Arran,*
Attacked in the late days of Confusion, a Bloody, Popular,
and Formidable Error in its Camp, Fortified and Defended 70
by all the strength of *England;* and for ever secur'd his
own, and so much of the Publick reputation as was entrusted
to him; managing that charge with the same Wisdom, Justice,
and Fidelity he has done the Kingdom of *Ireland,* and many
other great Commands, for the Honour and Service of the
King. In the Young Earl of *Ossery* we have great assurances,
the Grandfather and Father shall live in him, and receive the
last rewards of Vertue Men are capable of in this World,
to have their Honour and Happiness extend beyond their own
beings. And herein the History of your Grace seems a Com- 80
ment on the Fifth Commandment, you have always Honoured
the Father of your Country, and your Days of Honour continue
long in the Land, in your own Person, and your Illustrious
Race. A useful President to *England.*

That I may approve my self an honest and grateful
English-man, is one reason of my Address: I have also other
obligations on me. Your Grace has been a Princely patron
and encourager of Poetry; a Pleasant but Barren Country
where my Genius and inclination has cast me. I am entangled
among the Inchantments of it, though it affords nothing but 90
a good Ayre, a little vain reputation, and we must climb for
it, and shall miss it too, if envy or ill nature can hinder us.

67   'em] 3   e'm   1, 2
90   Inchantments]   Hvd, Mich 1   inclinations   USC, LC, Prin, Yale,
Penn, Vas 1, 2, 3

There were no living, if some great Men elevated not only
in Quality but Understanding above the rest of the World,
did not Protect us from these *Barbarians,* because they know
us. I beseech your Grace then give me leave to pay my Duty
to you. Many and great are your Revenues in Honour, in the
Camp, the Court, the Church, and the whole Common-wealth
of Learning. The Poet may be employed as well as the Histo-
rian. I have made but a small Collection, but I have put it in 100
hands that I hope will not soon embezle it. This Comedy has
rais'd it self such a fortune in the World, I believe it will not
soon run away. Give it leave to Honour it self with your great
Name, and me with
the Title of,

> *May it please your Grace,*
> > *Your Graces most*
> > > *Humble and*
> > > > *Obedient Servant.*
> > > > John Crown.

The Prologue.   A3

What are the Charmes, by which these happy Isles
Hence gain'd Heaven's brightest and eternal smiles?
What Nation upon Earth besides our own,
But by a loss like ours had been undone?
Ten Ages scarce such Royal worths display
As *England* lost, and found in one strange Day.
One hour in sorrow and confusion hurld.
And yet the next the envy of the World.
Nay we are blest, in spite of us 'tis known,
Heavens choice for Us was better than our own.   10
To stop the blessings that oreflow this day,
What heaps o' Rogues we pild up in the way?
We chose fit tooles against all good to strive,
The sawciest, lewdest, Protestants alive.
They wou'd have form'd a blessed Church indeed,
Upon a Turn-coate Doctor's lying Creed.
To know if e'er he took Degree is hard,
'Tis thought he'l have one in the *Palace* Yard,
Plot swallowers sure will Drink no more stuff down,
From that foul Pitcher when his Ears are gone.   20
Let us rely on Conscience, not on Cheats,
On Heavens wisdom, not on Juglers feats.
How greatly Heaven has our great loss supplyed?
'Tis no small Vertue heales a Wound so wide.
Nay in so little time to reer our Head,   A3ᵛ
To our own wonder, and our Neighbours dread.
They see that Valour Crown'd with regal Power,
They oft have seen with Lawrels Crown'd before.
Verse is too narrow for so Great a Name,

    2   Hence]   1, 2, 3   Have   1b
    5   worths]   1, 2   Worths   3   :   worth   1b
    17 e'er]   3   e're   1, 1b, 2
    22 not on Juglers]   1, 2, 3   not State-Juglers   1b
    23 our great loss]   1, 2, 3   our loss   1b
    28 oft have seen with Lawrels]   have oft seen with Lawrels   1b:
oft have seen what Lawrels   1, 2, 3

Far sounding Seas hourly repeat His Fame.   30
Our Neighbours vanquish'd Fleets oft wafted o'er
His Name to theirs and many a trembling Shore;
And we may go by His great Conduct led
As far in Fame as our Forefathers did.
At home he milder ways to Glory chose,
God like, by Patience he subdued his Foes;
Now they and their designs are Ruin'd all,
Beneath their fallen, accurst, Excluding Wall.
These are not all the blessings of this Isle,
Heaven on our Nation in a Queen does smile.   40
Whose Vertues, Grac'd by Beauty, shine so bright,
All the Fair Sex to Vertue She'l invite;
And all the Clouds turn to a glorious Day,
By that Illustrious paire's united ray,
Who both Reform and Grace Us by their sway.

31   o'er] 3   o're   1, 1b, 2
40   does] 1, 2, 3   doth   1b
41   Vertues, Grac'd] 1b   Vertue's Grace   1, 2, 3
43   the Clouds] 1, 2, 3   our Clouds   1b
44   by that] 1, 2, 3   by this   1b

A   **B**

COMEDY

Call'd

Sir Courtly Nice:

or,

It Cannot Be.

Act. I

Scene, Lord Bellguard's *House.*

Enter at several Doors Leonora *and* Violante.

LEO. My Dear –   (*They embrace.*)

VIO. My Dear, how is it with thee? What amendment in
thy Brothers humor, and thy condition?

LEO. None.

VIO. Oh! thou break'st my heart, for I love him extreamly, and am, I think, as well belov'd by him; but whil'st
he has this Disease upon him so mortal to Liberty, dare
venture on him no more, than if he had the Plague, or 10
any other Distemper dangerous to Life. For what is life
without Liberty? To be his Wife is worse than to be a
Ghost, for that walks and enjoys a little chat sometimes,
but I must be laid by a Conjurer call'd a Husband for my
whole life, I would not be a Queen on the tearms; no nor
on any tearms, because a Queen is confin'd to Forms, so
fond am I of Liberty; but next to that I love your Brother;
I wou'd give all the World to cure him, is there no
way?

LEO. None that I know of.   20 **B**ᵛ

VIO. Must we then be for ever unhappy, I in the loss of
him, and you in Eternal Slavery?

LEO. I might have Liberty, but on such tearms –

1-2 Order of lines reversed in 1, 2, 3
20 of] 3   off 1, 2

Vio. What Tearms?

Leo. Marriage with such a Coxcomb, you know him – Sir
Courtly Nice.

Vio. A tempting Man, he has a vast estate.

Leo. But incumber'd.

Vio. With what?

Leo. A Fop, 'tis morgag'd to a thousand expensive Follies, 30
if it were not, I wou'd not drink water for the sake of a fine
Bowl chain'd to the Well. The Youth I love has a fair and
free Estate.

Vio. Mr. *Farewel* is it not?

Leo. The same.

Vio. Ay, but he's forbidden Fruit.

Leo. I know it to my sorrow.

Vio. What's the reason?

Leo. History must tell you. There has been a pique between our Families since the Conquest; none were thought 40
truly of our Blood, that had not that Scurvy in it; because
mine began to sweeten, my Father almost suspected my Legiti-
macy; and left me no Fortune but on condition I retain'd the
Ancient mark of our House.

Vio. There arises then your Brothers great Authority.
He has the disposal of your Fortune, by consequence of
your Person; Fortune is all Men seek now. They are so
cow'd from Marriage, they will go Voluntiers into a Battle
but must be prest to marriage; and 'tis the Shilling
does it.   50

Leo. Too true, But I believe Mr. *Farewel* of a more
generous temper, he addresses still.

Vio. It may be he does not know how it is with you,
you have the Fame of Ten thousand pound.

Leo. And the Money too, if I marry with my Brothers
consent, not else.

Vio. That's hard, but Mr. *Farewel* has enough for you
both.

Leo. Ay, if he will venture on me; yet if he will I know
not how to come at him, I am so watch'd, not only at home 60

but abroad. I never stir out but as they say the Devil does, with Chains and Torments. She that is my Hell at home, is so abroad.

Vio. A new Woman.

Leo. No, an old Woman, or rather an old Devil; nay worse than an old Devil, an old Maid.

Vio. Oh! there's no Fiend so envious.

Leo. Right, she will no more let young People sin, than the Devil will let 'em be sav'd, out of envy to their happiness.　　70

Vio. Who is she?

Leo. One of my own Blood, an Aunt.

Vio. I know her, she of thy bloud? she has not had a drop of it, these Twenty Years; the Devil of envy suck'd it all out, and left verjuice in the roome.

Leo. True, this Aunt hangs on me like a daily Ague; but　B2
I had rather endure her, then be cur'd by such a nonsensical Charm as Sr. *Courtly* is. And nothing else can be applyed to me; for to assist my governing Aunt, there is a whole Army of Spies in the House; and over them two Spies Gen- 80
eral: And there my Brother thinks he shews a Masterpiece of Policy.

Vio. Why? what are they?

Leo. Two, that will agree in nothing but one anothers confusion. The one is a poor Kinsman of ours, so fierce an Enemy to Fanaticks, that he cou'd eat no other meat; and he need no other Fire than himself to roast 'em, for he's always in a flame when he comes near 'em, his Name is *Hot-head.*

Vio. And I warrant thee the other is a Fanatick.　　90

Leo. Oh! a most Zealous Scrupulous one; with a conscience swadled so hard in its Infancy by strict Education, and now Thump'd and Cudgel'd so sore with daily Sermons and Lectures, that the weak ricketty thing can endure nothing.

76　All copies of 1 are signed *E2*.

VIO. Certainly these two, must make you sport.

LEO. Oh! their faces, Dresses, Names are jests. The Fanat-ick's Name's *Testimony*.

HOT. (*Within.*) Where is my Lord? Where's my Lord?

LEO. Oh! I hear my Cholerick Cousin *Hot-head*.   100

Enter Hot-head.

HOT. Where's my Lord? Where's my Lord, I say?

LEO. What wou'd you do with my Lord?

HOT. Call him to an account if he were not my Cousin, cut his pate, it may be Cudgel him. Heaven be thank'd to Cudgel a Lord is no *Scandalum Magnatum*.

LEO. What's the reason of all this anger?

HOT. He affront's me, he invites me to live in his house, and then keeps a Fanatick to make a jest o' me. He knows I sweat when I see one.   110

LEO. May be he has occasion for one.

HOT. What occasion? He is not in a Plot, is he? Fanaticks are good for nothing else that I know of.

LEO. Why not? Toads are good for something.

HOT. Ay, when they are hang'd and dryed, so is no Fanat-ick. He is such a canker'd Rogue, he does mischief when he's hang'd; let him spread Ink upon Paper and it raises blisters. But here the Rogue is.

Enter Testimony.

Sirrah! Sirrah! What's your business in this House, 120 Sirrah?

TEST. What Authority have you to examine me, Friend?

HOT. Friend, you Dog! call me Friend, I'le knock you down Sirrah.

TEST. Poor Soul – poor Soul –

HOT. You are an Impudent Rascal to call me poor Soul – Sirrah, I have a Loyalty and a good Conscience, and that's a better Estate, than any / of your Party have; and if you   B2ᵛ live in the House with me, I'le settle it on you with a Pox to you.   130

TEST. Yes, Mr. *Hot-head* I know you well enough, I know you would hang us all if you could.

Hot. I need not Sirrah, for Heaven be prais'd now you begin to hang your selves; I knew when *Tyburn* was bestow'd upon the Priests and Jesuits, the Fanaticks and Republicans wou'd not long be without it, for they are very fond of all Church Lands, come, Sirrah, if you live here, I'le make you turn over a new leaf, I'le make you go to Church, Sirrah.

Test. That's more than you do your self Mr. *Hot-head,* 140 you go not often to Church.

Hot. What then? I'm for the Church, Sirrah. But you are against the Church, and against the Ministers, Sirrah.

Test. I cannot be Edifyed by 'em, they are formal, weak, ignorant, poor Souls – Lord help 'em – poor Souls.

Hot. Ignorant? you're an impudent Rascal to call Men o' their Learning Ignorant; there's not one in a hundred of 'em, but has taken all his Degrees at *Oxford,* and is a Doctor, you Sot you.   150

Test. What signifies *Oxford?* can't we be sav'd unless we go to *Oxford?*

Hot. *Oxford* don't lye out o' the road to Heaven; you Ass.

Test. Pray what do they learn at Oxford? only to study Heathens; they'l talk of *Aristotle* in the publick, they may be asham'd to name *Aristotle* among civil People.

Hot. Oh! you Sot.

Test. Our Ministers are powerful Men. (*To* Leonora.) Oh! Forsooth I wish you were under one of our Ministers; you 160 wou'd find they wou'd pierce you forsooth; they wou'd go to your inward parts.

Hot. This Rogue is talking Bawdy.

Test. They would shew you the great – great sinfulness of sin, that sin is one of the sinfullest things in the whole World.

Hot. You senceless Rascal, what should be sinful but sin? what should be foolish but a Fool?

Leo. Are not these a ridiculous Couple?

TEST. Come, this is very provoking, and very Prophane; 170
I shall have a sad time on't in this wicked Family.

HOT. Wicked! Sirrah: What wickedness do you see in this
Family?

LEO. Ay, Mr. *Testimony,* now we are all concern'd, what
Vices do you find among us?

TEST. Suppose I see not many Vices, morality is not the
thing; the Heathens had morality, and forsooth would you
have your Coachman or your Footman to be no better Men
than *Seneca?*

HOT. A Coachman a better Man then *Seneca?*   180

LEO. I wou'd have him be a better Coachman than I believe
Seneca was.

TEST. Ay, and a better Christian too, or woe be to him.
But truly I see great wantonness even in your self forsooth,
the very Cook debauches you.

HOT. How? call the Cook! Cook! Cook!   B

LEO. The Cook debauch me, Sirrah?

TEST. I mean by pampring you, Morning, Noon, and Night
with one wanton kickshaw or another.

VIO. You Coxcomb.   190

LEO. Sot.

HOT. Rascal, I thought the Cook had layn with my Cousin
– Sirrah, you deserve to have your bones broke. Well Sirrah,
since you find my Lords Table is too lusty, I'le have it
guelded; I'le make you keep *Lent,* and fast *Wednesdays* and
Fridays.

TEST. I will not, I abhor it, 'tis Popery.

HOT. Then you shall fast *Tuesdays* and *Thursdays.*

TEST. And then the Family will slander me, and say I do it
out o' contradiction – I will not do it, I do not love to grieve 200
the weak.

HOT. To grieve the strong thou mean'st, thy own strong
stomack.

TEST. You are offensive.

HOT. I will be more. I will watch you Sirrah, and know
why my Lord feeds such Rascals.

TEST. I tarry not for his feeding, the Family is a sad Family, and I tarry out of pure Bowels.

HOT. Out of empty Bowels, which you have a mind to fill, and it may be you may fill other empty bellys, I mean among 210 the Wenches, some of you Godly Rogues play such tricks some times. I'le watch you Sirrah.   (*Exit.*)

TEST. And I'le watch you, my Spirit rises at this Man exceedingly.   (*Exit.*)

VIO. These are a pleasant Couple.

LEO. Is not my Brother politick? These are to see no Provisions for wantonness be conveigh'd to me from abroad, and be sure they will not agree to deceive him. And that I may have none at home, My Brother will not venture a handsome Servant in the house; he swears he will not be 220 Brother in Law to e'er a Butler or Footman in *England;* and he has cull'd for his Family, the most choice peices of deformity he cou'd find in the Nation. I believe they are now altogether in the Pantry, and my Aunt among 'em distributing their Breakfasts – the Monsters will be worth seeing – open the Door.

> *The Scene is drawn, and a Company of Crooked,*
> *Wither'd, ill-look'd Fellows are at break-*
> *fast, and* Aunt *with them.*

AUNT. How now? Who open'd the Door without my 230 leave? Neice, this is one o' your Girlish tricks, will you always be a Child? Will you never learn staidness and gravity, notwithstanding the perpetual Counsel you have from me, the perpetual displeasure I shew at all sort of youthful Follies; do not you know how I hate impertinent Youth?

LEO. (*Aside.*) Or any sort o' youth to my knowledge.

AU. Do not I always tell you how fine a thing it is to be Grave; that Youth with Gravity is very passable, and almost esteem'd equal with years? Very wise Persons 240 will not be asham'd to match with Grave Youth; daily experience shews it, and will you never leave? Fye – fye –

221 e'er] 3   er'e 1,2

fye – I / wou'd not for the World any Wise Sober Person   B3
o' Quality that has an Inclination for you, shou'd ha' seen
this rudeness in you, to Expose your Aunt in this manner,
in her undress; it might ha' created in him an aversion for
you.

LEO. (*Aside*). An aversion to me, to see your ill
dress?

AU. Madam, I hope you'l pardon the liberty I take in 250
your presence.

VIO. Oh! good Madam.

AU. Oh! Madam – pardon me – I know I commit a Sole-
cism in good Manners, but you are a Lady that has a great
deal o' goodness, and a great deal o' worth –

VIO. Oh! sweet Madam!

AU. Oh! Madam! our Family has found it – you are
pleas'd to Honour us with your Friendship. We may venture
to expose our Frailties before you, Madam, you'l be so good
to pardon – Madam –   260

VIO. Oh! Madam!

AU. Well really Madam – I wonder where my Neice learns
her wantonness, we are the most reserv'd Family in the
World. There were Fourteen Sisters of us, and not one of us
married.

VIO. Is't possible?

LEO. (*Aside.*) To your great grief –

AU. We were all so reserv'd. Oh! Madam! no Man durst
presume to think of us; I never had three love Letters sent
to me in my whole life.   270

VIO. Oh! strange!

AU. Oh! we were very reserv'd. Well Madam I am very
much out o' Countenance to appear thus before you.

VIO. Oh! Madam, every thing becomes you Madam.

AU. Oh! you are very obliging Madam. Do you hear Neece
– learn o' this Lady?

LEO. (*Aside.*) To flatter you –

257 you are pleas'd to] 1, 2   you pleas'd us to 3
266 Is't] 3   I'st 1, 2

AU. Madam I am extream unfortunate, the affairs o' the
Family call me away from your sweet Conversation.

VIO. The misfortune is mine, Madam.   280

AU. Oh! sweet Madam your most humble Servant.

VIO. Your humbler Servant dear Madam. (*Exit* Aunt.)
Ha! ha! ha! what ridiculous peice of Antiquity is this? Thy
Brother has a great Honour for his Family since he will keep
such a relick of his Ancestors as this.

LEO. All the house is of a piece.

VIO. Nay if thou learn'st lewdness at home, thou hast a
great Genius to it.

LEO. Well, what do you think of my condition?

VIO. I like it.   290

LEO. Like it?

VIO. Ay, for I perceive your Brother has put the whole
force of his Wit into this Form of Government; now if we
can baffle it, he will find it is a dream fit for nothing but
Utopia; and never torment himself and his Friends with it
any more, then he'l be a faultless Creature, and all of us
happy in our Loves. Here he comes.

Enter Lord Bellguard.   B4

Your Servant good my Lord.

BELL. Your most humble Servant Madam.   300

LEO. My Lord, why do you call him Lord? he's a Doctor
and curing me o' the Palpitation o' the heart, Falling-
sickness, Convulsions in the Eyes, and other such Distem-
pers.

VIO. A Doctor? a Quack by his false Medicines; short-
ly we shall see him mount the Stage, or stand at the *Old
Exchange* and cry a Cure for your Horns, a Cure for your
Horns.

BELL. I'm glad to see you so pleasant Madam.

VIO. How can I otherwise chuse my Lord, and see your 310
Family and Government?

BELL. Faith, Madam he that will have a Garden must

282 humbler] 1, 2   humble 3
306 *Old Exchange*]   *Old----Exchange* 1, 2, 3

inclose it, and cover tender Plants: This is a very blasting age
to Vertue, 'twill not thrive without a covering.

VIO.   Ay, but my Lord, you force your ground too much,
what Horns wou'd not grow in your Soyle? When wou'd not
your Forehead sprout? Were I your Wife and thus kept, I
shou'd spread like a Vine, and all the Walls in *England* wou'd
not hold me.

BELL.   I'm not o' that opinion, Madam.   320

VIO.   Why shou'd you think better o' me than your Sister?

BELL.   I judge very well of her, but must speak freely I
think few Women may be trusted in this life, this World is,
and ever was a great brothel; where? or with whom may a
Woman be trusted? with ancient Ladies; they are the chief
Beauty Merchants, venders of fine Love.

LEO.   Ladies o' that Profession.

BELL.   Oh! the most excellent, and most in Employ. Ped-
ling Women cry Scotch Cloath of a groat a yard, stuff only
fit for Footmen. But wou'd you have fine Beauty, Choice of 330
Beauty, and with ease Security and Decency, go to your Lady
Merchants; in Common houses the work is manag'd as slovenly as Religion in Conventicles, enough to put one out of
conceit with it; but in Brothels o' Quality, Iniquity is carried
on with that venerable order wou'd intice any one to Devotion.

VIO.   Fye! fye!

BELL.   And with that security. A Man may there enjoy a
Lady whilst her Husband holds her Cards.

LEO.   And shall the Lady o' the house know o' these
things?   340

BELL.   And manage 'em too; break the Lady to the Lovers
hands; that's the advantage o' Quality, if a young Lady has
not a natural amble, a poor Bawd cannot have access to
teach her.

VIO.   What can a Lady o' Quality propound by such
doings?

BELL.   Oh! many things. As Presents; and Pleasures. She
has her house full of good Company, her Ears full of wanton

346   doings] 1, 2   things 3

Stories; her Eye full of tempting Sights, and now and then
her Lips get a close kiss. Oh! Madam! do you think it 350
does not warm an Elderly Lady's blood, to have a brisk
young Spark always by her side? he is her Liquour of life,
and though she never gets a full draught, a tast chears her
heart.

LEO. Who are these Ladies? where do they live?   B4ᵛ

BELL. Oh! you'd feign be acquainted with 'em? no such
matter; and yet I'le tell you where they live.

LEO. Where?

BELL. Almost every where; where there is an Amorous
Aunt, or over-indulgent Mother.   360

LEO. Mothers? will Mothers corrupt their Daughters?

BELL. Ay, or if they wont Daughters will corrupt their
Mothers. Things are so inverted, that Ladies who were honest
all their Youth to be like their Mothers, turn lewd in their
old Age to be like their Daughters. There never was such
an open and general War made on Virtue; young ones of
Thirteen will pickeere at it, and by that time they are twenty,
they are risen to be Strumpets General, and march in publick
with their Baggage, with Miss, and Mass, and Nurse and Maid,
and a whole train of Reformade sinners, expecting the next 370
Cully that falls.

VIO. You talk of paltry husses.

BELL. Very good Gentlewomen.

LEO. Gentlewomen o' those employments.

BELL. Ay, purchase 'em. I have known a fair young Lady
give all her Fortune to attend a Man o' Quality in his Bed-
Chamber; be his chief Gentlewoman.

LEO. Suppose so, what's all this to me? If they be bad must
I be so?

BELL. Truly Sister, a rambling Woman let her be never 380
so good a manager, will be apt to bring her Vertue as a Travel-
ler does his Money, from a Broad peice to a brass Farthing:
But say she does not, is reputation nothing? and let me tell
you, Reputation will hang loose upon a galloping Lady; you
may as well go among high Winds and not be ruffled, as

among Men and not have your good Name blown over your Ears.

VIO. Those Winds blow where they list. A Woman is not secure at home from Censure.

BELL. But you must allow a Jewel is not so safe in a Crowd 390 as when lock'd up.

LEO. Lock'd up? do you think to lock me up?

BELL. I think to secure thee, my dear Sister.
Woman like Cheney shou'd be kept with care,
One flaw debase's her to common Ware. (*Exit.*)

Act II.

Scene Violante's *house. Enter* Violante
and a Servant.

VIO. Is Mr. *Farewel* coming?

SER. Yes Madam, he's just at the Door.

VIO. That's well, if this brisk young Fellow, has but Love enough to undertake this work, and Wit enough to go through with it, we shall all be happy.

Enter Farewel.

FA. [*To* Servant.] Where's your Lady? Madam, your most humble Servant.   10

VIO. Your Servant Mr. *Farewel*; you are a happy Man, young, rich, and in the Ladies Favours.

FA. I'm glad to hear that, Madam; who are these Ladies Madam? a day, an hour of Youth and good Fortune is precious; and Ladies like Birds must be aim'd at whilst they hop about us, miss that opportunity you may loose 'em for ever. Therefore the Ladies, good Madam, quick, quick, for if you defer but half an hour, they'l be in love with some body else.

390 Crowd] 3   Crow'd 1, 2
394 *Woman*]   *Women* 1, 2, 3
14 a day, an hour]   a day, and hour 1, 2, 3

Vio. No Mr. *Farewel,* there is one Lady more Constant, 20
you'l own it when I name her; my Lord *Belguard's* delicate
young Sister. What say you to her?

Fa. I adore her.

Vio. And dare you attempt her?

Fa. Dare I?

Vio. Ay, for do not you know you are the only Man forbidden her.

Fa. Do I know of what Race I am, Madam? Never was
such a pack of Fops as my Lord *Belguard's* Ancestors and
mine. They lov'd wrangling more than we do intriguing; 30
kept Lawyers instead o' Wenches, and begot upon their
bodies, a thousand illegitimate Law Suits, the Terms they
observ'd as duly as the River does the Tydes, and Land
was carried too and frow, as mud is in the Thames. Nor
were their quarrels so bitter about Land, as place; so big
were their great hearts, they cou'd not come into one Room
together, for fear of loosing place. My Lord *Belguard's*
Father to end the difference, most piously endeavour'd to
be a better Man than any of his Ancestors. That is to say
a Lord.   40

Vio. And then the strife ended?

Fa. Was more enflam'd. For my Lord was more insolent,
as having Authority under the Broad Seal to be proud, by
Consequence my Father more enrag'd; and both the old
Gentlemen contended who shou'd have the greatest Estate
in malice, and attain'd to be very considerable, and when
/ they dyed, endeavourd to settle it all upon us. But truly   Cᵛ
the young Lady and I most prodigally consum'd all our
Portions at one look, and agreed to cut off the wicked
Entail.   50

Vio. You did well, but how will you accomplish your
desires? her Brother has such guards upon her.

Fa. Oh! 'tis Decreed! nor shall thy Fate oh! Brother!
resist my Vow, though Guards were set on Guards, till

38 endeavour'd]   endeavours 1, 2, 3
49 off] 2   of 1, 3

their confounded Coxcombs reach'd the Skies, I'd o'er 'em
all –

VIO. You are in a Rapture.

FA. Ten thousand when ever I think of her.

VIO. But how will you do this?

FA. I have leagu'd with a Witch; at least a young Fellow   60
that has more tricks than a Witch; he was a poor Scholler at
Oxford, but expell'd for studying the Black Arts.

VIO. For Conjuring?

FA. Yes, Madam, not only any Mans Pigs or Poultry,
but Wife or Daughter into his Chamber. Nothing cou'd scape
him, and he scap'd every thing. The Proctors watch'd more
diligently for him, then a Benefice, and cou'd never catch him.
The Grave Doctors abhor'd him worse than a Haeresie, and
studied more to keep him out of their Families, but he con-
futed their Skill, and they cou'd no more light upon him than   70
on a jest.

VIO. I long to see him.

FA. I ordered him to come hither to me.

Enter a Servant.

SER. Here's one Mr. *Crack* enquires for you, Sir.

FA. That's he – bring him in.

Enter Crack.

Mr. *Crack* your Servant.

CR. Your Servant Sir, your humble Servant, Madam.

VIO. Your Servant Sir, I am told you ha' been an *Oxford*   80
Scholler.

CR. A Scholler Madam? a Schollers Egg – emptied by
old suck-Eggs, of all that Nature gave me, and crumbled
full of Essences, Hypostases, and other stuff o' their baking.

VIO. Why did not you apply your self to Divinity?

CR. Leave Wenches for Pigs, Madam; 'tis true I may
Wench then too, but it must be with Fear and Reverence, I
hate that.

VIO. Why wou'd not you be a Physician?

CR. A Gold-finder Madam? look into Jakes for bits o'   90

55 o'er] 3   or'e 1, 2

money? I had a Spirit above it. I had an ambition to be of some honourable profession; such as People of Quality undertake. As for instance, Pimping. A Pimp is as much above a Doctor, as a Cook is above a Scullion; when a Pimp has foul'd a Dish, a Doctor scours it.

VIO. This is an arch Blade.

CR. Oh! you are pleas'd to say so, Madam; 'tis more your goodness than my desert.   C2

FA. Well Mr. *Crack,* you know what you have undertaken.   100

CR. I'le do't – The Lady's yours. Give me some Mony.

FA. There, there.

CR. Gold, thou Son o' the *Sun,* and Brother o' the *Stars,* Nutmeg o' comfort, and Rose o' delight, as my Friend the King o' *Persia* call's himself, what can'st thou not do great Prince, if I be thy chief Minister? (*Exit.*)

VIO. This is a notable Fellow, our next Plot must be to secure your Rival Sr. *Courtly Nice.*

FA. Hang him, he secure's himself by his Foppery's, she despises him.   110

VIO. Not many Lady's do so.

FA. Oh! no, Madam, he's the General Guitarre o' the Town, inlay'd with every thing Women fancy; Gaytry, Gallantry, Delicacy, Nicety, Courtesy.

VIO. And pray, put in Gold too.

FA. True Madam, Oh! the Ladies love to have him in their Chambers, and play themselves a sleep with him.

VIO. Well, I have provided one shall thrumble on him.

FA. Who's that?

VIO. *Surley.*   120

FA. Oh! Fire and Water are not so contrary, Sr. *Courtly* is so civil a Creature, and so respectful to every thing belongs to a Gentleman, he stand's bare to his own Perewig. *Surly* uncovers to nothing but his own Nightcap, nor to that if he be drunk, for he sleeps in his Hat. Sr. *Courtly* is so gentle a Creature, he writes a challenge in the stile of a Billet-doux. *Surley* talks to his Mistress, as he wou'd to a Hector that wins

his Mony. Sr. *Courtly* is so pleas'd with his own Person, his
daily contemplation, nay his Salvation is a Lookinglass, for
there he finds Eternal happyness. *Surley's* Heaven, at least, 130
his Priest is his Claret Glass; for to that he confesses all his
Sins, and from it receives Absolution and Comfort. But his
damnation is a Looking glass, for there he finds an Eternal
fire in his Nose. In short if you wou'd make a Posset for the
Devil, mingle these two, for there never was so sweet a thing
as Sr. *Courtley,* so sower as *Surley.* But how will you get
'em together? for nothing has power over *Surley*, but Claret
and the Devil.

VIO. Yes I have. Heaven is pleas'd to think the Devil
himself has not mischief enough to plague that ill-natur'd 140
Rogue, and joyns me in Commission with him to torment him
with Love; he loves me.

FA. Love? can he love?

VIO. So much, he neglects his Claret for me; and comes
hither hourly to perform his Devotions to me, but in such a
slovenly manner; 'tis such a *Non-Conformist* to all decent
Ceremonies.

SURLEY. (*Within.*) Where's your Mistress?

VIO. I hear him, we'l ha' sport with him. He abhors
his Love worse than / Murder or Treason, for those are 150 C2ᵛ
mischiefs to others, but Love he accounts High-Treason against
his own damnable Person; and he's more asham'd of it, than
he wou'd be of a Beasts Taile if it grew out of him. Therefore
I'le conceal, and do you charge him with it, you shall hear
how he'l renounce it, then will I appear like Conscience to
a sick debauch, and you shall see what an aukard Penitent I'le
make him.

Enter Surly.

FA. Honest *Surly,* how do'st do?

SUR. Prethee look in my Water. 160

FA. In thy Water?

SUR. Ay, for I don't love to answer impertinent questions.

130   Heaven, at least, his Priest]   2   Heaven at least, his Priest   1, 3

FA. Is it impertinent to enquire after the health of a Friend?

SUR. A Friend? thy talk is more boyish than thy Face. Do'st thou think there are such Friends? thou believ'st there are Mair-maids and Centaures I warrant; for such Friends. Monsters that grow to some other Beasts, and are the least part o' themselves?

FA. Why? hast thou no concern for any Beasts but thy self? 170

SUR. Yes Bird, for many things for my own sake; for Witty Men whil'st they drink with me, handsome Whores whil'st they lye with me, Dogs, Horses or Cattle whil'st they belong to me; after that, I care not if the Wits be hang'd, the Whores be pox'd, and all the Cattle bewitch'd.

FA. A very generous temper.

SUR. 'Tis a wise and honest temper. The pretended good nature is ill nature; it makes a Man an Ass to others, he bears their Burden, a Rogue to himself, he cheats himself of his quiet and Fortune. I am so very honest to my self, if the 180 whole World were hang'd it shou'd not rob me of a Minutes ease, I thank Heaven for it.

FA. Was ever such a Barbarian?

SUR. Thou'rt an Ass; which is the *Barbarian,* he that eats Man, or the Man that's eaten? The Rogue that grieves away my Flesh eats me, and is a *Barbarian*; so is he that with vexation gnawes himself; I am no such Cannibal.

FA. Hast thou no compassion?

SUR. I know not what it is.

FA. Suppose you see a Man o' Quality in Misery.   190

SUR. Let him be in misery and be damn'd.

FA. Are you not concern'd for his Quality?

SUR. The less for that, because if he fancies the whimsey he has it to please him.

FA. To trouble him.

SUR. Then to comfort him I'le tell him he's the Son of a Whore, and his Grandfather rose by Pimping.

FA. Suppose you saw a Man o' parts unfortunate?

SUR. Let his parts look after him.

178   others, he   3   others he   1, 2

FA. They'l afflict him.   200

SUR. Then to quiet him I'le tell him he's an Ass.

FA. Have you no charity? do you never give any thing to   C:
the Poor?

SUR. As much as any Man.

FA. What's that?

SUR. Nothing.

FA. Does no Man give any thing?

SUR. Not to the Poor; they give it to themselves; some
Fools have Diseases in their Natures, they never see any one
in pain, but they feel half on't, and so they give money to ease 210
themselves.

FA. Ha' you no love for any thing?

SUR. I have Appetite.

FA. Have you no love for Women?

SUR. I ha' Lust.

FA. No Love?

SUR. That's the same thing, the word Love is a Fig-Leaf
to cover the naked sence, a fashion brought up by *Eve,* the
Mother of Jilts, she Cuckolded her Husband with the *Serpent*
then pretended to modesty and fell a making Plackets presently. 220
And her Daughters take up the Trade, you may import what
Lewdness you will into their Common-wealth, if you will wash
it over with some fine Name. You may proclaime at Mercat-
cross, how great an Adorer you are of such a Womans Charms?
how much you desire to be admitted into her Service; that is,
how lusty a Centaur you are, that the Horse in you is much the
major part, and she shall receive all this without a blush,
whil'st the Beast trots to her under the Name of a Lover; when
if she had any Wit she'd know, a Lover is a more impudent
Name than Whoremaster; for a Whoremaster throws all his 230
Bombes at a whole City, your Lover wasts all his upon a single
House. That when a Woman desires a Lover, she desires to
have the whole Brute to her self.

223 Mercat-] 1   Markat- 2   : Merkat- 3
229 a Lover is a more impudent Name] 1   a Lover is a more impudent name 2   : a Lover is more impudent than a Whoremaster 3

FA. Ha! ha! ha!

SUR. What do you laugh at Sir?

FA. Only that your Mistress has heard your learned Discourses Sir. Pray appear Madam, and own you have lost your Wager, is he a Lover or no?

Enter Violante.

SUR. Here's a young Treacherous Rogue.   240

VIO. Yes – a Brutal one – are these your Sentiments of Love Sir? was it this you meant when you talk'd of Love? when we grow Lovers do we degenerate into Brutes? I thought there was a generous Passion, of which a Beast cou'd have no more sence, than he has of Musick or Poetry. And to such Love you pretended Sir.

SUR. (*Aside to* Fa.) I'le whedle her. So I do still Madam, but why must I let a Boy Catechise me? I have that Musical, Poetical, Fantastical love, you speak of, and a pox on me for it; you'l neither be my Slipper, nor my Shooe, my Wench 250 to slip on and off at pleasure, nor my Wife, that is a Whore buckled on.

VIO. You are charming in your expressions.

FA. Mr. *Surly,* Madam, is a mistical peice, to be understood like a Prophecy, where Rams and He-Goats stand for Kings and Princes. Mr. *Surly's,* rank expressions must signifie Virtue and Honour.

VIO. No, no, they signifie his own filthy meaning; and   C3ᵛ
the truth is, love has no other sence, in this corrupt Age. Now if a Woman by blushes or otherwise, confesses she 260 thinks a Man, a fine Gentleman, he to requite her sends her presently a Libel call'd a Billet-doux, where he in fine words tells her to her Face, he thinks her a Wench, and invites her to lye with him. This ruins all Conversation, Men are always driving their brutal appetites to the Plays, the Court, to Church, like Drovers their Beasts to every Market; and there's

no conversing with 'em, unless you'l take their Cattel off their hands.

SUR. Madam, I love you in your own fashion, admire you, adore you, and the Devil and all, what wou'd you have? (*Aside* 270 *to* Fare.) Now will this simple Jade believe me?

FA. He calls you simple Jade, Madam, and says you'l believe him.

SUR. You Malapert Boy, why do you meddle in my business?

FA. 'Tis my business, she's my Friend, and I wont see her abus'd.

SUR. A Friend to the Woman loves your Enemy, Tom-Fool?

FA. No, she hates him, and has quarrel'd with him, and 280 I wou'd ha' had you step into his room.

SUR. Oh! ho!

FA. Now who's the Tom-Fool?

SUR. I am, look you Madam, that Rogue despayr made me talk like an Ass, and I am sorry for it.

VIO. I know you are Sir, I know your base desire is, for your punishment, confin'd to my Eyes, and I'le use you as you deserve.

FA. Come, Madam, let me interpose; though you will not receive Mr. *Surly* as a half Horse, you may as a whole Ass, 290 a Drudge, you know you have business most agreeable to his ill Nature, pray employ him.

VIO. Well; I'le make tryal of him, you pretend you love me Generously.

SUR. Yes, and Damnably.

VIO. Know then my Lord *Belguard,* is (as I have of late perceiv'd) sunk with the rest of the Age, into base opinions of Love and Women, that I am angry I ever had a good thought of him.

267 off] 2, 3   of 1
282 Oh! ho!] 1   Oh! oh 2, 3
286 is, for...punishment,]   is for...punishment; 1, 2, 3

Sur. Good.   300

Vio. Look upon his address to me, as an affront, and will
revenge it.

Sur. Better and better.

Vio. And you shall do it.

Sur. Best of all.

Vio. Do not you know Sir *Courtly Nice*?

Sur. That you shou'd joyn knowledge with such a Fop?
'tis a question to be put to a Boy? I may know Philosophy,
but to ask a Man if he knows a Horn-Book? for such a
thing is this Fop; guilded on the out side, on the inside, 310
the Criss Cross row, and always hanging at the Girdle of a
Girl.

Vio. You have describ'd him right. This Fop has my
Lord *Belguard* entic'd to accept his Sister with no Fortune,
but her Birth and Beauty. Now if you'l break the Match,
you'l be to me the most amiable Creature in the World.

Sur. Or the most damnable, if you Jilt me.   C4

Vio. In earnest of a farther favour here's my hand.

Sur. There's the Devil in it. Tis transforming my shape,
I am growing a Womans Ass, I feel the Ears prick out o' 320
my skin already; and I must hoof it away with her load of
Folly upon my back. Well I am thy Ass at present, but if thou
Jilts me, I will be thy Devil. (*Exit.*)

Vio. 'Tis the fittest Office for thee; thou art so like one
already, you may pass for Twins. Now Mr. *Farewel* let's go
in and Laugh.   (*Exit.*)

       Scene Lord Belguards *House. Enter* Hot-head
                and Testimony.

Test. He shall not speak with her, I don't approve of it.

Hot. You approve Sirrah? what ha' you to do?   330

Test. I have Authority.

Hot. You Authority?

Test. Yes, from my Lord.

Hot. You had it then out of his Kitchin, Sirrah; the Beef
o' the Nation breeds all the Maggots in the Peoples heads.
I am sometimes tempted to throw down their Porridge-pots,

and spill the Divine Right of Presbitery. In short my Lord
is a man of honour, and you have belyed him, Sirrah.

TEST. It is well known I make a Conscience.

HOT. Ay, you Rogues making o' Consciences is a great 340
trade among your Party, and you deserve to loose your Ears
for it.

TEST. I mean I keep a Conscience.

HOT. Y'ave reason Sirrah, it keeps you; but that an honest
Lord shou'd give money for a Rogues false Conscience –
Oones!

TEST. Well but don't swear.

HOT. Sirrah, who swears?

TEST. De'e hear? don't swear I say.

HOT. Oones! Sirrah, don't preach to me.   350

TEST. Don't swear then.

HOT. Sirrah, if you preach to me, I'le cut your Pate.

TEST. Had I a Sword 'twere more than you cou'd do.

HOT. How now Sirrah? (*Takes* Test. *by the throat.*)

TEST. Nay, but don't throttle me, don't *Godfrey* me.

Enter Aunt.

AUNT. What's the noyse? what's the rudeness, Cousin *Hothead?* you a Gentleman, and make a Bear-Garden of a Person
of Honours house?

HOT. Better make a Bear-garden of it than a Conventicle; 360
here's a Fanatick Rogue ordain'd ruling elder o' th' Family
by my Lord, as the Rogue says, so he undertakes to govern
and Preach.

AU. And you undertake to Govern and correct? Cousin
no body Governs here but I; if he had committed faults, you
shou'd have brought him before me.

HOT. Oh! you'd have him enter'd in your Office?

AU. What do you mean? obscenely? you are confident.
You are the first / Gentleman that offer'd to say a wanton   C4ᵛ
thing to me.   370

349 De'e] 3   Dee 1, 2
358 Person] 2, 3   Persons 1
367 enter'd in] 1, 2   enter'd into 3

Hot. (*Aside*.) To your great sorrow.

Enter Leonora.

Leo. What 's the quarrel here?

Hot. There's a Taylor wou'd fain speak with you.

Leo. All this noyse to introduce a Taylor?

Hot. He can't get through this Fellows narrow Conscience, yet there is room for a whole Common-wealth.

Au. Call in the Taylor; there must no Cloaths be made without my orders, that I may see 'em modest.

Leo. (*Aside*). A Taylor? I order'd no Taylor.   380

Enter Crack.

Au. How now, Sir? what are you?

Cr. A Taylor, Madam.

Au. Who sent you? I know you not.

Cr. Your own Taylor, Mr. *Stitch,* Madam.

Au. How chance he came not himself?

Cr. He's sick, Madam.

Au. And can you work well, for we are very hard to please? There's scarce a Taylor in Town can make me endure to see my self.   390

Leo. (*Aside*.) The fault lyes in Fifty – Fifty.

Cr. Indeed Madam, I must needs say my Country men are not the best Taylors in the World. This is a fine Nation, and all spoyl'd by the Taylors. Heaven makes the Women Angels, and Taylors make 'em Hedg-hogs; 'tis a sad sight to see 'em, now I'le make an Angel of a crooked Pin.

Au. Where did you learn your Skill?

Cr. In *France,* Madam.

Test. In *France*? then Friend I believe you are a Papist.

Hot. Sirrah, I believe you are a Presbyterian.   400

Test. Friend, if you be a Papist I'le ha' you before a Justice.

Hot. Sirrah, if you be a Presbyterian, I'le kick you down Stairs.

379 'em] 1, 2   them 3
394 makes the Women] 1, 2   makes Women 3
397 Where] M. Summers   Ay, where 1, 2, 3

TEST. What are you Friend?

HOT. Ay, what are you Sirrah?

CR. What am I? why, I'm a Taylor, I think the Men are mad.

AU. Intolerable; Mr. *Testimony,* pray leave us, and Cousin *Hot-head,* I shall desire the same of you, unless you'l behave 410 your self like a Gentleman.

HOT. I will behave my self like a Gentleman, for I'le know of my Lord when he comes home, if he has given this Rogue Authority over me; if he has I'le demand Satisfaction of him; if he be innocent woe be to your prick-ears, Sirrah.

TEST. I fear you not.   (*Exit* Hot.)

AU. Mr. *Testimony,* I once more desire you'l give us liberty.

TEST. Yes, Forsooth, I dare trust the young Gentlewoman with you, For/sooth – you are a grave – Gentlewoman and in 420 D years – Forsooth.

AU. In years, rude Clown.

TEST. And truly she's a very pretty sweet Woman, and deserves to have great care taken of her.

LEO. Well Sir, we'l excuse the care at this time.

TEST. (*Aside.*) Pretty Woman.

LEO. Pray leave us.

TEST. [*Aside.*] Sweet Woman – I profess she's strangely alluring, I had best retire least I fall into frailty, and be discovered.   (*Exit.*) 430

CR. Now, Madam, before I take measure of you, I'l shew you some Patterns – (*To the* Aunt.) please you to look upon some Madam, you have judgment.

AU. Let me see.

CR. To you, Madam, I wou'd recommend this peice.

LEO. Mr. *Farewel's* Picture? Oh! ay Sirrah! now I guess thee – my Dear – Dear –   (*Kisses the Picture.*)

CR. Have a care o' your *Aunt* Madam. I have a Letter too.

LEO. Give it me – quick – quick –   440

436 ay Sirrah!]   I Sirrah! 1, 2, 3

Au. These are pretty Silks.

Cr. The best in *France,* Madam.

Bell. (*Within.*) Where's my Sister?

Leo. My Brother? I hope he does not know thee.

Cr. No, if he does I'm a dead Man.

Leo. Hast thou no disguise for fear he shou'd?

Cr. Only this great pair of Spectacles.

Enter Lord Belguard.

Bell. What Fellow's this?

Leo. A Taylor.   450

Bell. Not your Taylor?

Au. No, he's sick and sent this Fellow in his Room.

Bell. How comes such a young Fellow to wear Spectacles?

Cr. Young, my Lord? I'm above Five and Fifty.

Bell. Thou bear'st thy age well.

Cr. Ay, every where but in my Eyes I thank Heaven.

Bell. [*Aside.*] This Fellow may be a Bawd for ought I
know, I'le watch him.   (*Exit.*)

> Aunt *views the Patterns,* Bell. *stands behind*
> *his Sister, and watches* Cr. Cr. *mean while*   460
> *puts his Measure before, and delivers*
> *her a Letter.*

Cr. Well, Madam, I perceive your Ladyship likes the
Pattern I shew'd you first.

Leo. I have seen the whole piece.

Cr. And your Ladyship likes it?

Leo. Oh! very well.   D�

Cr. I'le assure you, Madam, you'l like it mightily when
'tis upon you, and you have a sweet body to work for. I do
not doubt, Madam, but to get a great deal o' credit and a 470
great deal o' Custome by you, among the Ladies, as soon as
ever they see my work.

Leo. Well, let's see your work, and I'le say something.

Cr. That you shall and speedily, Madam, I'le bring you
home as sweet a peice o' Work, as ever you had in your Life.
You'l look upon the Pattern I shew'd you last?

Leo. Yes.

CR. That's for the inside; do you like much Bombast, Madam?

LEO. No.   480

CR. Well, Madam – I ha' taken a Surveigh o' your fine Body – now you shall be pleas'd according to your own hearts desire – your Servant Madam.   (*Exit.*)

BELL. Well Sister – prepare to receive a Visit from Sr. *Courtly Nice,* this afternoon.

AU. Oh! dear! then I must dress. He's a great Critick. (*Exit.*)

LEO. (*Aside.*) She designs him for her self, wou'd she cou'd get him.

BELL. Sr. *Courtly* and I have agreed; pray give him your 490 promise.

LEO. So soon? 'twill be fulsome, he's abstemious.

BELL. Therefore take him whil'st he has an edge.

LEO. You use to despise Fools, how chance you marry amongst 'em?

BELL. Because none but Fools will marrry. Wits are but few and commonly poor; Fools are numerous and rich. Fortune is as fond of those bits of Men, as Bigots are of Reliques; wraps 'em in Silver.

LEO. Better they were buryed. A Fool in a Coach is like a 500 Knave in a Pillory, the Object of publick derision.

BELL. Oh! there are few to deride 'em, many to admire 'em, so many, I have oft admired how one Apple,

> Shou'd such Diseases in old Adam breed,
> That from his Loyns not Men, but Worms
>   proceed.   (*Exeunt omnes.*)

Act III.   D2

Scene, Covent-Garden-Square. *Enter* Farewel
and Crack *meeting.*

FA. Oh! the News! the News! art thou an Angel or a Devil? bring'st thou Joys or Torments?

CR. Joys! joys! joys!

FA. Angel! Angel! Angel!

CR. In the first place I deliver'd your Picture.

FA. Rare.

CR. And she kissed it.

FA. Kissed it?   10

CR. Sweetly, wantonly, lasciviously. She set me so on fire,
I kiss'd all the Wenches as I came along, and made their moyst
lips fiz again.

FA. Oh! Rogue! Rogue! delicious Rogue.

CR. Then I deliver'd the Letter, and before her Brothers
face.

FA. Before his face? ha! ha! ha!

CR. Prepare this Night to be the happyest o' Mortals.
Give me some more Mony.

FA. Mony? I'le sell my Land rather than thou shalt want. 20
That one Inheritance will purchase me two, one in Love, and
another in laughing at this politick Brother.

CR. No, no Inheritances. As for laughing, I believe you
will have an Anuity for life; but for Love you'l only have a
lease for three or four Years.

FA. Pleasant Rogue! here's Money.

CR. So, so, I wish you joy, I wish you joy.   (*Exit.*)

FA. See *Surly* going to my Rival; my affair thrives ad-
mirably.   (*Exit.*)

Enter Surly. *Knocks, enter a* Servant.   30

SUR. Is *Nice* within?

SER. *Nice* Sir?

SUR. Ay, *Nice* Sir; is not your Masters name *Nice*?

SER. 'Tis Sir *Courtly Nice.*

SUR. Well Sir, If I have a mind to clip half his Name,
'tis not Treason, is it Sirrah?

SER. I believe not Sir.

11   so on fire] 1, 2   soon on fire   3
23   No, no Inheritances. As]   No, no Inheritances as   1, 2, 3
27   joy, I] 2, 3   joy I   1
32   Nice?] 3   Nice. 1, 2
35   a mind] 1, 3   a nid   2

SUR. Then get you in, and tell your Master I'd speak with him.

SER. What sort o' domineering Man is this?   40

Scene, a Chamber – Sir Courtly Nice *dressing,*   D2
Men and Women singing to him

Sir Co. Very fine! extreamly fine. Gentlemen and Ladies, will you do me the favour to walk in, and accept of a small Collation? I am in some hast to dress upon an extraordinary occasion. You'l Pardon me? your very humble Servant. (*Exit Musick*).

SER. Very fine.

Sir Co. You Sot, 'twas very barbarous.

SER. Your honour said 'twas very fine.   50

Sir Co. You Clown, don't you know what belongs to a Gentleman? Complaisance is the very thing of a Gentleman, The thing that shew's a Gentleman. Wherever I go, all the World cryes that's a Gentleman, my life on't a Gentleman; and when y'ave said a Gentleman, you have said all.

SER. Is there nothing else Sr. belongs to a Gentleman?

Sir Co. Yes, *Bon mine,* fine Hands, a Mouth well furnish'd –

SER. With fine Language –

Sir Co. Fine Teeth, you sot; fine Language belongs to Pedants and poor Fellows that live by their Wits. Men of 60 Quality are above Wit. 'Tis true for our diversion sometimes we write, but we ne'r regard Wit. I write but I never writ any Wit.

SER. How then Sir?

Sir Co. I write like a Gentleman, soft and easie.

SER. Does your Honour write any Plays?

Sir Co. No, that's Mechanick, I bestow some Garniture on Plays, as a Song or a Prologue.

SER. Then your Honour is only a Haberdasher o' small Wares?   70

Sir Co. A Haberdasher, you sawcy Rascal?

Enter a Servant.

49 'twas very barbarous] 1, 2   'twas barbarous 3
56 else Sr.] 1   else Sir 2 : else belongs 3

2. SER. Here's one Mr. *Surly* to visit your Honour.

Sir Co. *Surly,* what the Devil brings him hither?

2. SER. He has been walking about the Rooms this quarter of an hour, and wou'd not let me bring him in, till he had fould 'em all with his dirty Shoes.

Sir Co. A Nauseous, Beastly Sloven, Clown, Fool, Sot.
Enter Surly.

Dear Mr. *Surly* your most humble Servant. (*Sir* Co. *Bows to* 80
receive him.)

SUR. What, are you unbu – buckling my Shooe?
(Sur. *is Drunk, stammars and belches.*)

Sir Co. Dear Mr. Surly – (*Aside.*) he stinks horribly –
How came I to enjoy – (*Aside.*) a very Polecat – This great happyness? (*Aside.*) pox! foh! you and I have been long *piquee,* and I'm amaz'd to see you at my *levee.*

SUR. I begin to think, thou art a good honest Fellow, and   D3
have a mind we shou'd no longer be two lo – lo – Loggerheads,
but one.   90

Sir Co. Dear Sir, you are always so divertising; Well Sir, shall I beg a favour of you?

SUR. What's that?

SIR Co. Leave to dress before you, Sir. I am to meet some fine Women to day, one presently.

SUR. Prethee dress, and be damnd – shall we di – dine to-gether?

Sir Co. Yes Sir, I suppose, and Sup too.

SUR. That's kind, well when?

Sir Co. About Five o' clock Sir.   100

SUR. Where?

Sir Co. In the Kings Box, Sir.

SUR. Must you and I, dine in the Kings Box?

Sir Co. Oh! dearest! I beg your Pardon Ten thousand times, I thought you ask'd me where I shou'd meet the Lady.

SUR. Pox o' the Lady; I ask where we shall Dine?

Sir Co. Really Sir I don't know, I can't put my head into

78 Beastly Sloven]   Beastly, Sloven 1, 2, 3
91 divertising] 1, 2   diverting 3

one o' your beastly eating houses, nor swallow the filthy meat
you eat there, if you'd give me One hundred pound.

Sur. Filthy Meat? Sir I eat as good Meat as you do.   110

Sir Co. Oh! dear Mr. *Surly,* no doubt the meat in its own
nature may be very innocent; but when once it has committed
familiarity with the beastly Fists of Cooks and Butchers, 'tis
to me an unpardonable Sinner. My Butcher cuts up all his
Meat with a Fork.

Sur. Does he cut up an Ox with a Fork?

Sir Co. Ay, and he cuts up an Ox as neatly as a Lady does
a Partridge.

Sur. Well, then I'le accept o' thy Dinner.

Sir Co. Dear Sir, your most humble Servant; (*Aside.*) pox 120
on him. I wish I be capable o' the great happyness. For I came
but last Night from my Country house, and I question whether
I have all things in order or no. Whose there? are all things
brought from my Country house?

Ser. No Sir, your Butler has forgot your Salt.

Sir Co. Left my Salt? careless Rascal. Let him take Horse
immediately.

Ser. Sir he's rid post for it.

Sur. Rid post for Salt? whether?

Sir Co. To my Country house.   130

Sur. How far's that off?

Sir Co. But a little way, not above Forty miles.

Sur. Send Forty miles out o' *London* for Salt? Is there
not Salt enough in *London* for you?

Sir Co. Ay, stuff pawm'd by Butlers and Waiters, they take
up the Wenches coats, then handle the Salt.

Sur. (*Aside.*) Here's a Rogue – well come let's drink a
Glass o' Wine then.

Sir Co. Oh! dear Mr. *Surly,* if you name Wine, you
make me throw up my Soul. I have abhor'd Wine ever since 140
I was in *France,* and saw what / barbarous Education they   D3
give that generous Creature. Duce take me, Sir, if the Clowns

142   give]   1, 2   gave   3

don't press all the Grapes with their filthy naked Feet. Oh!
beastly nasty Dogs! no wonder we are poyson'd with their
Wine.

SUR.   Prethee what o' that? the Wine purges before it comes
over.

Sir Co.   Oh! Lord Mr. Surly what a Phrase is there? you'l
Pardon my Freedom, Sir?

SUR.   (*Aside.*) Most civil Coxcomb. Well what must we   150
drink, for drink I must?

Sir Co.   I have several drinks of my own composing at your
Service, as *Mead, Syder, Ale* –

SUR.   Ale? there's Sauce for a Woodcock. Come let's tast a
Bottle.

Sir Co.   [*To* Servant.] Fetch a Bottle; (*Aside.*) This Fellow
will Poyson me.

SUR.   Well I come to request a favour o' thee.

Sir Co.   Your most humble Servant Sir, how de'e like this
Cravat?   160

SUR.   What's that to my business? I come to make a request
to thee.

Sir Co.   'Tis well tyed too, with a great deal o' humour.

SUR.   A Pox on thee, mind me.

Sir Co.   Your most humble Servant Sir.

SUR.   I am going to make Love.

Sir Co.   Before you drink Sir?

SUR.   Before I drink Sir.

Sir Co.   Well Sir, since you'l have it so, I'le wait on you
down stairs.   170

SUR.   Is the Devil in the Fellow? I tell thee I'm going to
make love.

Sir Co.   Oh! Lord Sir, I beg your pardon a thousand
times.

SUR.   And I come to beg thy assistance.

Sir Co.   Oh! dear Sir.

SUR.   For thou hast a knack on't. Thou art the only Court

150   Coxcomb. Well]   Coxcomb (*aside*) well what   1, 2, 3
159   de'e]   3   de'e'   1, 2

Card Women love to play with; the very Pam at *Lantereloo,* the Knave that picks up all.

Sir Co. Oh! Sir, you are so obliging; (*Aside.*) and stinking 180 – Pox take him.

SUR. And 'tis a very pretty Woman I'm in love with; my Lord *Belguard's* Sister *Leonora*; thou know'st her.

Sir Co. (*Aside.*) The Rogue's my Rival, he was born for my confusion. Ay, Sir, I have the honour of some small acquaintance there.

SUR. Prethee speak for me.

Sir Co. Oh! dear Sir, you have a great Talent of your own.

SUR. But thine's a better. One thing I am sure thou may'st do, there's an abominable Fop makes Love to her, and I am 190 told is to marry her; prethee tell him he's a Son of a Whore.

Sir Co. Really Sir I'm unfortunate; I ha' no manner o' Genius to that sort o' Conversation.

SUR. Say my words. Tell him if he proceeds, I'le not only Libel him, but tweag him by the Nose, Kick him, Cudgel him, and run him through the Guts. Prethee tell him this. (*Hugs Sir* Co.)

Sir Co. Oh! pray Sir give me Ayr.

SUR. Prethee do.

Sir Co. Sir I am ready to –   200

SUR. And thou wilt tell the Puppy this?   D

Sir Co. I will upon my Soul.

   Enter a Servant *with Wine and Glasses.*

SUR. Then thou art an honest Fellow – so, is the drink come? fill a Glass, why two Glasses? do you think I cannot drink after your Master. (Sur. *flings away a Glass.*)

Sir Co. (*Aside.*) Pox o' your Complyment –

SUR. Here *Nice,* my Mistresses health.

Sir Co. (*Aside.*) What misery is this Beast imposing on me? he coughs in the Glass too –   210

SUR. Pox on't, a whole gulp went the wrong way, come off with it. 'Tis my Mistresses health.

Sir Co. (*Aside.*) This Fellows the Devil –

212 it. 'Tis] 2 it 'Tis 1: it, 'Tis 3

Sur. Off with it, Man.

Sir Co. I never was so embarass'd since I was born.

Sur. Oones! off with it.

Sir Co. (*Aside.*) I must take the beastly portion down, but
I shall be most horrible sick after it. (*Drinks.*)

Sur. So, now thou art an honest Fellow, now I'le kiss thee.

Sir Co. (*Aside.*) The Devil thou wilt? more miseries? nay 220
but Mr. *Surly.*

Sur. I swear I will.

Sir Co. Nay but you'l disorder me.

Sur. I swear I will.

Sir Co. But Sir I'm going upon your occasions to your
Mistress.

Sur. Nay then I'le give thee two kisses, one for thy self
and another for her.

Sir Co. (*Aside.*) Oh! Hell. Nay but Mr. *Surly.*

Sur. I swear I will. (*Kisses him and belches.*) This Bottle 230
Beer is damn'd windy – well honest *Nice* farewell to thee.
(*Exit.*)

Sir Co. Who's there? I'm sick to death – to death! lead me
in – get my bed ready – and a Bath – and some Perfumes
– I'm sick to death – I'm dead.   (*Exit.*)

      Scene Lord Belguard's *House. Enter* Bell.
         with Farewel's *Picture in his hand.*

Bell. Thou horrid Vision! wou'd I had met with the worst
Fiend in Hell, rather than thee; in thee there is a Legion ex-
citing me to Blood – blood – Who's there?   240

Enter a Servant.

Ser. My Lord –

Bell. My Coach – to blood – blood –

Enter Leonora *and* Aunt.   D4ᵛ

Leo. To Blood? what means my Brother?

Bell. Be gone.

Leo. To whom do you speak?

Au. Bless us; Nephew what ailes you?

Leo. Alas my Lord, I fear you are a going to quarrel.

227 thy self] 1, 2   my self   3

BELL. Yes, I'm going to punish one who Violates my 250
Fathers, my Will and calls my Mother Whore.

LEO. What execrable Wretch is that?

BELL. Thy self.

LEO. Me?

BELL. Yes, what dost thou else but proclaim our Mother
false, when she conceiv'd a thing so opposite to all our Fathers
race as thou art?

LEO. In what?

BELL. In Infamy; when was there a spot in our name, till
Heaven for our sins sent thee among us? and I am going to 260
destroy thee in thy lewd undoer.

LEO. I know of no reproach in our Family but your madness, destroy that. What are your Spyes and Coxcombs, but so
many Capital Letters, wherein you write over your Door, My
Sister is a wanton Woman.

BELL. 'Tis truth, you are not only a wanton, but a wicked
Woman; not only Intrigue, but with the Enemy of our Family,
Farewel.

AU. How?

LEO. (*Aside.*) I am betray'd –   270

BELL. Do you blush?

LEO. At your Folly.

BELL. Dare you deny it?

LEO. Who dare accuse me?

BELL. This Picture, which I found in your Chamber.

AU. Horrid Creature! I shall swoon away.

LEO. (*Aside.*) How shall I bring off this? All this noise
for a Picture? if you had found a little humane Effigies in
swadling Clouts, there might ha' been some squawling.

AU. Do you laugh at your shame?   280

BELL. She shall ha' no cause.

LEO. Do, kill me, before you know whether he's guilty
or no.

BELL. I'le know it from himself. If he denys it, it will
be some revenge to make him stab his Soul with Lyes. He shall

277   this?]   this (*Aside*) All...Picture?   1, 2, 3

swear not only that he never did, but never will send so much
as an Imagination to you.

LEO. Do, if you wou'd force him hither, what charm to
a Man of spirit, like daring?

BELL. (*Aside*.) She speaks sence in that.   290

LEO. If you wou'd be fighting, fight your own jealousie,
which abuses you worse than Mr. *Farewel* can do, my Honour
protects you from him; but neither Wit or Honour, can guard
you from the rude insolence of your jealousie, which is now
sending you of an Errant, a Footman o' Spirit wou'd scorn,
to proclaim the dishonour of your own Sister. Fye! Fye!

BELL. And so I must sit down tamely with this abuse?   E

LEO. You are not abus'd, the Picture was found at Church.

AU. At Church? do you intrigue at Church?

BELL. They do nothing else, the Church is almost as bad 300
as the Porch.

AU. Nay there's shameful doings, that's the truth on't, it
provokes my Flesh to see how the young Men fling their Eyes
about.

LEO. (*Aside*.) And not upon her.

AU. But 'tis no marvail; when Women will encourage 'em.
No Fellows dare gape upon me, because I never encourage
Fellows.

LEO. (*Aside*.) A Face of Fifty is small encouragement.

BELL. Nay no wonder the Devils cause thrives, he has a 310
numerous Clergy, Heaven has but one Minister in the Church,
and whil'st he is Preaching Divinity, the Devil has a thousand
of both Sexes, by all the Oratory of looks and dresses, preaching Fornication and Adultery.

AU. Too true, well she's certainly undone. I dare not
examine her Breasts, if there shou'd be any thing in 'em,
I shou'd dye.

LEO. In my breasts?

AU. Ay, Gentlewoman, do you think I regard your Flim
flam story o' the Church?   320

LEO. 'Tis not my story, my Woman found it in *Westminster Abby,* at Prayers, and I knowing what work wou'd

be made with it, commanded her to burn it, and she has dar'd
to dissobey me.

WOM. Indeed, Madam, I thought to have presented it to a
Friend o' mine; and laying it out o' my hand unfortunately
in your Honours Chamber, my Lord found it.

BELL. Oh! how nimbly she takes the lye at the first rebound?

AU. Out upon you; I'm extream sick – lead me in – not
you – you are not fit to touch a Woman o' my Virtue. These 330
things have strange impression upon me.   (*Exit.*)

LEO. (*Aside.*) That you don't share in 'em.

BELL. Pray, Sister, go out o' my sight, you are an horrour
to me.

LEO. Your own Dreams are. Y'are as mad as a Prophet,
you have always before your Eyes a Vision of Horns and
Whores.

BELL. All this goes upon the score of *Farewel's* heart blood
if he be guilty, I'le make enquiry presently, and search at what
gap this Treachery entred.   340

LEO. (*Aside.*) Oh! unfortunate negligence!   (*Exit.*)

Enter Hothead.

BELL. Who's there, Cousin *Hot-head, Testimony*?

HOT. Oh! are you here?

BELL. Ay, to your sorrow, if you have play'd me false.

HOT. You ha' serv'd me finely.

BELL. Do you first complain?

HOT. Coupled me with a Dog?

BELL. But you ha' Coupled my Sister Sir.   E

HOT. With a *Fanatick* Rogue.   350

BELL. No – with a finer Gentleman. Who brought this
Picture?

HOT. The common Fire-fork of Rebellion.

BELL. A Fire-fork. Fork me no Forks – Who brought this
Picture?

HOT. The rotten rump shou'd ha' been burnt – when 'twas
only Roasted.

BELL. The rotten Rump – Answer me, or I'le fight thee.

328 nimbly] 1, 2   nimble 3

Hot. Answer you what?

Bell. Who brought this Picture? I found it in my Sister's 360
Chamber.

Hot. Then your Fanatick Rogue conveigh'd it thither to
make me suspected, out of his malice to the Common-Prayer.
I'le cut the Rogue to peices.

Enter Testimony *with a great Sword by his*
side.

Bell. *Testimony.*

Test. I am here.

Bell. How now, Sworded?

Test. To preserve my Life. My life is threatned by that 370
bloody Papist.

Hot. How, Sirrah? dare you think of fighting me?

Test. Yes, and hope to do it, through Providence.

Bell. Drawing before me? (Hot. *and* Test. *offer to draw.*)

Hot. Will you protect a *Fanatick*? I see what you are.
Well Sirrah, though I may not cut your Throat, I'le choak you
Sirrah.

Test. De'e, hear the bloody Papist? He'l throttle me.

Hot. Sirrah, I'le cram the Oaths of Allegiance, and Supremacy into you, and they'l stick in your Throat, though 380
Treason wont, and so I'le to a Justice presently.   (*Exit.*)

Bell. And stay with him, and never plague me more. Now
Sir do you resolve my question.

Test. I do resolve I will not take the Oaths.

Bell. I do not ask you about the Oaths.

Test. Why, if you ask me Ten thousand times, I will not
take the Oaths.

Bell. Did one ever see such a Coxcomb?

Test. Call me what you please, I will not take the Oaths –
So do your worst.   (*Exit.*) 390

Bell. A very fine account of my business.

Enter a Servant.

Ser. My Lord a Gentleman desires to speak with your
Honour.

Bell. I'm not to be spoke with, I'm a broad – my Soul is

– in the heart of *Farewel,* ripping it up for this Secret. What Gentleman?

SER.   One from th' *East-Indies,* My Lord, he brings a Letter from your Uncle *Rich.*

BELL.   He comes in a Storm; he will find worse Weather 400 E here, than any he met at Sea. But I'le endeavour to compose my self – admit him.

Enter a Man *drest like a Merchant.*

MAN.   My Lord, your Lordships most humble Servant. I perceive your Lordship has forgot me; you will know me better, when I acquaint you, who I am. My Father had the honour of being a Retainer to your Lordships Father, of Honourable memory; and sent me some Years since to the *East Indies,* in the Service of your Noble Uncle, Mr. *Rich.* My name is *Waytewel.* 410

BELL.   Oh! Mr. *Waytewel,* I am glad to see you, truly you are so chang'd, if you had not told me who you was, I shou'd never ha' known you.

MAN.   I believe so my Lord – (*Aside.*) for I'm sure you never saw my Face before, but the Picture of it you have – for *Waytewel* was my Picture. Time and Travels will alter a Man, but truly I have lost nothing by my Travels but my Countenance; and in the room have gotten what's better, a convenient small competency of some Seven or Eight thousand pound; Heaven and your Uncles love be prais'd. I have brought 420 Your Lordship some Letters from your Noble Uncle, and a small Present of some Threescore thousand pound.

BELL.   How?

MAN.   Only the trouble of it, my Lord. Your Uncle contracted in th' *Indies* an intimate Friendship with Sir *Nicholas Calico,* President for the *East India* Company. Sir *Nicholas* dyed, and left most part of his Estate (which was near a Hundred thousand pound), to his only Son, Sir *Thomas.* But poor Sir *Thomas* happen'd in his Fathers Life time to fall into a Distemper, which gave him a scurvy flaw in his Brain, 430 that Sir *Nicholas* left him and all his Estate to your Uncles Guardianship. Now your Noble Uncle perceiving his affairs

are like to detain him many Years in th' *Indies,* and fearing
if he shou'd dye, poor Sir *Thomas* might be cheated of all;
he has like a Worthy and honest Gentleman, sent Sir *Thomas*
and all his Estate to your Lordships care, as these Letters will
testifie. I suppose your Lordship is well acquainted with your
Uncles Hand and Seal.

BELL. I am, and this is his Hand and Seal – (*Reads.*)
um – um – um – to preserve him from being cheated here, 440
or beg'd in *England,* I take the boldness to recommend him,
to the care of so Noble a Person as your Lordship – um – um
– um –. Well Sir the Letter expresses what you told me. Where
is the Gentleman.

MAN. I brought him along with me; he's in the next
room, my Lord. Poor Gentleman, he has the oddest Phrases
and ways with him. He will needs be attended like a great
Indian Mandarine, or Lord. And has brought with him several
Siamites and *Bantammers,* that serve him as his Slaves, in
the ridiculous Dresses and Modes of their own Countries. 450
We had such a gaping Rabble after us, as we came along.

BELL. Pray call him in, I long to see him.

MAN. Sir *Thomas* – pray come to my Lord.

Enter Crack *ridiculously drest, attended by Men,*   E2ᵛ
in the Habits of Siamites, *and* Bantammers.

CR. Which is the Peer?

MAN. This is my Lord.

CR. Great Peer, your extream humble Servant.

BELL. Your Servant Sir, you are recommended to me, by
my Uncle.   460

CR. I know it my Lord, and am most incomparably
oblig'd to him. He is a Person, my Lord, that as to the altitudes
of Friendship, and the most glorious Circumstances of a Singular Person, is not to be cast up by the Logarithmes of
Oratory, nor his Latitude to be taken by the quadrangle of
Circumlocution.

BELL. [*Aside.*] So – I find I shall ha' store o' Non-sence.

---

439   Seal–(*Reads.*)]   Seal reads– 1, 3 : Seal, reads– 2

CR. My Lord, I'm a Person that as to the Circumstances
of Mony, am not indifferently contemptible; and as to the
circumstances of Honour, I am by profession a Merchant, by 470
Generation a Knight. Sir *Nicholas Calico* applying his Person
to my Mother, was the Author of, Sir, Your humble Servant.

BELL. So the Letter says.

CR. The Letter contains Verity.

BELL. [*Aside.*] Pox! I shall be teaz'd.

CR. One thing more Sir, I am a Person that as to understanding, am under the circumstances of Witchcraft. I lov'd
in th' *Indies,* a fair Christian Curiosity, and a nauseous *Indian*
Baggage, had a mind to apply to my Person her Tawny Circumstances; and finding she cou'd not obtain her Ambition, 480
applys her self to an *Indian* Bawd, and Bewitches me.

BELL. (*Aside.*) Pshaw! Bewitch! what stuffs here?

CR. Bewitches me Sir, what follow's thereupon? a loathing
in me of Females? I abhor Women; fall into Agonys when I see
Women. Pray let me see no Women.

BELL. You shall not Sir.

CR. Pray My Lord, no Women.

BELL. I'le warrant you Sir.

CR. But as much Supper as you please, my Lord.

BELL. You shall Sir.   490

CR. You are highly civiliz'd.

MAN. I told Your Honour he had such odd ways; well
My Lord, as soon as the Ship is come up the River, which will
be in few days, I'le bring the Captain to wait upon Your
Lordship, with the account of Sir *Thomas* his Estate, Aboard;
which will amount to Forty thousand pound, besides Ten
thousand pound he has brought a shore in rough Diamonds.
So, My Lord, your very humble Servant. Sir *Thomas* your
Servant, I leave you in good hands.

CR. Your Servant, Sir.   500

BELL. I'le order things for you. [*Aside.*] I must dispose

475   Pox!]   Pox I   1, 2, 3
476   as to understanding]   1, 2   as to your understanding   3
499   Servant, I]   2, 3   Servant I   1

this Man quickly, for I'm horribly weary of him, and also impatient to go about my Affairs.

[*Enter* Leonora.]

LEO. 'Tis he – I'm sure 'tis he –   (Leo. *peeps.*)   E3

BELL. How now Sister? what's your business here?

LEO. Staring at this strange sort o' Man.

BELL. You were no Woman else – pray get from him speedily.

LEO. You are not jealous of a Mad-man sure? he's mad is 510 he not?

BELL. Yes, and impertinently brings me vexation too from the *Indies,* at a time when I've enough at home, as every Man has, that keeps a Woman. Pray get from him, he hates to see Women.   (*Exit.*)

LEO. Hates to see Women? ha! ha! Sir Thomas *Calico* your humble Servant, you are welcome from the *Indies*; but have a care of being discover'd, least you be under the circumstances of a Cudgel.

CR. Truly Madam, I expect to have something stick by 520 my ribs presently, that is to say a good Supper; which I have order'd. My Lord and I will sup together, and you and Mr. *Farewel.*

LEO. We sup together? where? in the Grave? a fatall accident has hap'ned, will bring us both thither. My Brother has found Mr. *Farewel's* Picture in my Chamber.

CR. He shall not keep it, he shall deliver both Picture and jealousie.

LEO. Then thou art a Master. I told him my Woman found it in *Westminster-Abby;* may be thou may'st make something 530 out o' that?

CR. Stay let me consider *Westminster-Abby,* or the *Abby* of *Westminster* – um – um – Let me alone – begone – he comes.   (*Exit* Leo.)

Enter Bell.

525 has hap'ned]   has' hapned 1 : has hapned 2   has happened 3

BELL. Come Sir, let me wait on you to your Chamber.

CR. Hold, my Lord, a word, I have business of great consequence, I must humbly apply to your understanding.

BELL. (*Aside*.) So, I must be hindred with more Non-sence.

CR. I've in the *Indies,* a delicate peice of my Fathers Rib, 540
I beg your Lordship to advise me in the disposal.

BELL. Oh! dispose it how you please, Sir.

CR. 'Tis a Sister I mean, Sir.

BELL. Oh! that's something.

CR. She's sweet and slender as a Clove, and is worth two
Millions o' Coxcombs – Three hundred of 'em comes to Three
Farthings; 'tis a *Chinese* Mony. This Mony makes her much
sought in Marriage: The great *Hobbommoccoes* o' the *Indies*
come gallopping upon Elephants, Camels, Rhinoceroses, and
Oxen to see her. Now my Father was under the circumstances 550
of great obligation, to a Gentleman in *England*; and out o'
gratitude to him, ordered me on his Death bed, to bestow my
Sister on his Son, and Heir, if his actions have any sort o' smile
in 'em to his incompatible Father, which is the query. Pray
resolve it.

BELL. First let me know the Gentleman.

CR. You shall, I'le give you a Map of his Face, a Picture
contain'd in my pocket – ha! I ha' lost it – I ha' lost it.

BELL. Tell me his Name, Sir.

CR. I ha' dropt it out o' my pocket.   560

BELL. Ay, but his Name.   E3ᵛ

CR. I ha' dropt it out o' my pocket.

BELL. Ha' you dropt his Name out o' your pocket? His
Name Sir?

CR. Oh! his Name, I'le tell you both his Name, and Cogname. His Name is *Andrew,* his Cogname *Farewel.*

BELL. *Farewel*? what comes into my head? Sir can you
guess where you might loose this Picture?

549 come] 1, 2   comes 3
550 the circumstances] 1, 2   Circumstances 3
561 Ay]   I 1, 2, 3
567 can you] 1, 2   can't you 3

CR. A guess may be obtain'd – by the Prayers of Marriners.

BELL. No other way? those I seldome hear of.   570

CR. I was drawn down – stay let me see – remembrance begins to be idle – has *London* no place in the West?

BELL. Ay, no doubt.

CR. Ay, but something very West? something call'd West?

BELL. Yes – there's *West-Smithfield*.

CR. That's not th' appellative. Is there no Monster in the West, call'd Westmonster?

BELL. *Westminster* I believe you mean.

CR. Y'ave nick'd it. To *Westminster* I rode, to behold the Glorious circumstances o' the Dead; and diving into my 580 pocket, to present the represener with a Gratification, I am fully confirm'd, I then lost it; for my Eyes and the Picture had never any rencounter since.

BELL. [*Aside.*] This exactly agrees with my Sisters story, what a Prodigious thing is this? a discovery o' my Sisters innocence, sent to me from th' *Indies,* in a heap o' Non-sence? and in so Critical a minute; excellent Providence?

CR. What's an excellent Providence, Sir, that I ha' lost my Picture?

BELL. No Sir, that I ha' found your Picture.   590

CR. Found my Picture?

BELL. Ay, Sir, 'twas found by a Friend o' mine, in *Westminster-Abby* – there it is –

CR. Oh! my Picture! my Picture! my Picture!

BELL. Oh! my eas'd heart!

CR. Oh! my Picture! my Picture! my pretty Picture! My Lord I must requite this favour, [*To* Servant.] open that Casket, and give my Lord a handful of Diamonds.

BELL. A handful o' Diamonds.

CR. Ay, my Lord, I beg your Pardon for the inconsiderable- 600 ness o' the Present.

BELL. Inconsiderableness? what a Market wou'd some make o' this Man? put up your Diamonds.

CR. By no means, my Lord.

BELL. Put 'em up Sir, or you'l dissoblige me.

CR. You overwhelm me with Favours, I wish I had you at my house in *Bantam*.

BELL. I thank you, Sir; we are better where we are.

CR. My Lord, you put me under the circumstance o' blushing.   610

BELL. Pray let me put you into a Chamber, to rest your self.

CR. Rest is good – yours humbly –

BELL. Yours as humbly – What a Fire did I kindle in my   E4 house, to clear the Air of a Pestilence, was not in it? my Sister and all my Family are innocent. But what a fantastick thing is Womens Honour?

> *Whil'st She enjoy it, 'tis not seen or known,*
> *And yet when lost She's utterly undone.*

                        (*Exeunt Omnes.*) 620

Act IV   E4ᵛ

The Scene continues. Enter Violante *and*
Leonora *laughing.*

VIO. Ha! ha! ha! what an excellent Fellow is this? what Engines he has in his head? not only to wind himself into my Lords house, but the Picture out of his hands?

LEO. He undertakes to bring Mr. *Farewel* hither to Night. If he engag'd to bring him in a Church with a Parson to marry us, I wou'd not doubt it.

VIO. Certainly my Lord must be in a most mortified humour; now is the time to scarify him, and take out his 10 Worm.

LEO. Here he comes, now will I carry my self with all the insolence of a Vertuous Woman.

Enter Lord Belguard.

So my Lord, have your Slaves been gathering any more scatter'd smiles o' mine? what loads o' that Gold Sand have your Asses brought home?

618 *enjoy*] 1   *enjoys* 2, 3

BELL. [*Aside.*] They have heard all, now I am asham'd
to shew my Face.

VIO. Come, my Lord, wou'd you confine a Woman of 20
Honour? give her Liberty; wou'd you corrupt her? confine
her.

LEO. 'Tis true; were I a Wife to such a Man, I shou'd
abuse him out o' Pride; and think my self not an ill but
a great Woman, since to punish is a mark of Princely
Dignity.

BELL. This I confess is the English Dialect; and when
I talk of Governing Women, I talk of a thing not understood
by our Nation. I admire how it came about, that we who
are of all Nations, the most wise and free in other respects, 30
shou'd be the only Slaves and Fools to Women.

VIO. Oh! you are the Wisest of all Nations, you know
let Men do what they can, Women will do what they please;
and whereas other Nations by their spyes and Governantes
are at great toyle and charges to be Cuckolds, you have it
for nothing.

LEO. Come Brother, do not dress me in a Fools Coat,
nor hang spyes about me, like so many gingling Bells, to
give notice of all my motions. I can count, and know that
one and one, put shamefully together, are two lewd Fools, 40
and not one happy pair, as ill Women reckon, and deceive
themselves.

BELL. Sister, I believe you Virtuous, but I wou'd have
you not only be Virtuous but thought so. And truly a Woman
may be Virtuous, but is sel / dome wise in Mens company.   F
Her vain honour will put her on new Conquests. And Womens
Conquests are pretty things; they often end like those of
Highway Men, in a shameful Execution on their own Persons.
And yet all the business of their lives is mustering up Forces.
To day the Beauty Lyes ambush'd in undresses, the hair pin'd 50
up in Papers, like Serpents coyl'd to fly on you with greater
force; the Garments are loose and flowing as the Sea, to shew

38   like so many]   1, 2   like many   3
48   own]   2, 3   one   1

a *Venus* is there. To morrow she's as regularly fortified as a
Low Country Town, and oft a party of Charming looks are
sent abroad to put all Spectators under a contribution.

VIO. Your Wife must not dress?

BELL. Why shou'd she? I think Womens Poynts and Em-
broyderies, but so many Billet-doux in Needle work.

VIO. She must not go abroad or see a play.

BELL. Yes, She may go to Plays, provided she'l see Plays   60
and not Fools, it may be enter into Conversation with 'em,
and instead of getting Wit from the Plays, get folly from
the Fops; and so her Wit being spoyl'd in her Youth, shall
like a Clock set wrong in the Morning, go false all the day
after. In short, no Wife or Sister of mine shall dabble in
conversation with any Man; I hate a Slattern in her credit.

Enter Surly *peeping*.

SUR. (*Aside*.) I' my conscience I think I hear *Belguard* and
his Mistress quarrel in good earnest.

VIO. Let no Woman marry a Man o' your humour, but   70
she that for her Crimes is condemn'd to Transportation. The
Slave that in *Virginia* toyls to plant her Lord Tobacco, is not
more miserable, than she that in your bosome Labours to
plant a good opinion; both drudge for smoke. I scorn the
slavery, nor will marry a King to encrease his Dominions, but
to share 'em.

BELL. I offer you the entire Dominion o' my self; only
desire you, not to aim at further conquests.

VIO. I shou'd be a fine Soveraign, where Jealousie, Pride,
Rage, and such a sawcy Committee shall give me Laws; which   80
they wou'd never do to a Prince they lov'd.

BELL. I think I've given convinceing Proofs of Love.

VIO. When?

BELL. When I offer'd, Madam, to take you for better and
for worse; those are Heroical Complements. The form of
Matrimony out-does *Ovid* for passionate expressions.

VIO. Ay, my Lord, but that's none o' your Wit, and I

63   shall like a Clock]   1, 3   and like a Clock   2
84   better and]   1, 2   better or   3

wou'd not have a Man o' your parts, steal other Mens Phrases;
so Your Lordships humble Servant. Come away Child.

(*Exit* Vio. *and* Leo.) 90

Enter Surly.

SUR. Rare! they'r parted; once a Woman spoke truth.
My Lord, your Servant. I've overheard your quarrel, and I
honour you, you are the only Man in the Nation that understands himself. Lock up the Women till they'r musty, better
they shou'd have a Hogo, than their Reputations. And their
Honours are not like their Smocks, whitened by lying abroad.   F^v

BELL. Nor have their ador'd Faces the more esteem, for
often appearing.

SUR. Pox on 'em, they varnish like Copper, and the Women 100
are sensible of it, that's the reason they forge new faces every
time they go abroad; and all the Arts of Paint and dress are
suborn'd to give a Bastard beauty Title to Reign, because the
Legitimate Face is fallen into contempt by familiarity. No more
to be said, keep your ground like a Man of honour; (*Aside.*)
and loose your Mistress like a Coxcomb.   (*Exit.*)

Enter a Servant.

SER. An't please your Honour, Mr. *Hothead* and Mr.
Testimony, are return'd, as your Honour gave order.

Enter Testimony.   110

BELL. That's well – come Mr. *Testimony;* here has been
a mistake gave me a harsh opinion of you – I'm sorry for it.

TEST. Oh! My Lord, have a care of censuring Professors –
for a Professor.

BELL. Nay, prethee don't profess too much. I am satisfied
with thee.

TEST. Truly you would, if you knew of what a tender
Spirit I am of. I was only deluded the other day into a
Play-house, and truly it will be a burden to my Spirit whilst
I live.   120

BELL. A lack a day, well I hope you'l be the more tender
of my Sister, your trouble will not be long. I have engag'd

109   order] 1, 3   orders 2

her to a Gentleman, whom about this time I expect. What a clock is it?

TEST. Truly I do believe it is about Four, I cannot say it positively; for I wou'd not tell a Lye for the whole World.

[*Exit.*]

BELL. This is an excellent Fellow, if he be what he pretends. (*Knocking.*) Hark! some one at the Door – may be 'tis he – see –   130

Enter Hothead.

HOT. Did you send for me, my Lord?

BELL. Ay, Cousin, to reconcile my self to thee; I was in a mistake.

HOT. I think you was, when you judg'd a Rascally *Fanatick* a better Man than I.

BELL. The contrary Cousin – I think thee so much the better Man, I keep thee to have an eye over him, because I don't know if he be a Knave.

HOT. Not know if a *Fanatick* be a Knave? You'r fit to 140 sit in the House o' Peers i'faith.

BELL. Well, thou art a very honest Fellow Cousin – let me have thy Company. But what are those Patches on thy Face, for Ornament?

HOT. They are for Plaisters, but they are Ornaments. I have been in a *Fanatick* Coffee-House, and this is the Beauty they gave me.

BELL. 'Twas to reward some honourable Names, thou   F2
gav'st 'em.

HOT. I gave 'em no wrong names. I call'd 'em Rogues 150 indeed, but that's their proper Name; and they all set their hands to it immediately, and subscribed themselves Rogues upon my Chops, the only true Narrative they ever writ.

BELL. Thou art a mad Fellow – prethee go in.

Exit Hot. *at one Door. Enter at another* Testimony.

BELL. Well – who's at the Door?

TEST. A lamentable Soul.

141   Peers i'faith]   Peers I faith   1, 2, 3

BELL. A Beggar?

TEST. A more sad Object; but I conceive he comes rather
to rob than beg, for he comes Arm'd with a strong Bow and 160
Arrows.

BELL. A Bow and Arrows? what, is he a *Tartar*?

TEST. A Bow and Arrows made of Ribons, Laces, and
other idle Vanities, wherewith he intends to wound your Sister's
heart.

BELL. Oh! the canting Coxcomb.

TEST. Nay, why canting Coxcomb?

BELL. Be gone you senceless Ass; and bring in the Gentleman.

TEST. Nay, why senceless Ass? this is unseemly.   170

BELL. He wont stir.

TEST. I am no senceless Person – I ha' more sences than
your self; I have a sence o' Vanity, and of the nothingness
o' the things o' this World – and a sence o' Sin, and a sence
o' the insinuating nature o' sin – I dare not bring this wanton
frothy young Man to your Sister – for she is frothy also –
and sin will get in at a little crany – and if sin once get in his
head, he'l get in all his whole body. Now your honour has not
that sence o' these things you ought to have. That your Honour
is a senceless Person –   180

BELL. How Sirrah?

TEST. In a spiritual sence.

BELL. There's no getting this preaching Fellow away.
Cousin *Hothead*.

Enter Hothead.

HOT. My Lord.

BELL. Why do you let this canting Coxcomb plague me?

HOT. Why do you keep such a canting Coxcomb? let him
plague you, Pox you, and Damn you, I dont care.

TEST. Oh! sad! oh! sad!   190

HOT. Oh! shad! oh! Sot!

---

160   than beg] 1, 2   than to beg   3
179   things you ought to have.] That   2   things. You ought to have
that   1   :   things. You ought to have that: 3

BELL. So, now I've brought 'em both upon me.

HOT. He's always tuning his Nose, too high too low, like a Sowgelders Horn.

BELL. Well, Sir, if you please, tell me who's at my Door?

HOT. *Forty One* is coming in ding dong.

BELL. Into My Door? who's at my Door, I say?

HOT. *Old Forty One,* i'faith.

BELL. I cannot have an answer – Sirrah – who's at my Door?   200

TEST. *Popery,* I'm sure is coming in.   F2

BELL. Into my Door? I ask you, who's at my Door?

TEST. *Popery* I'm sure.

HOT. Roguery I'm sure.

TEST. *Popery* I'm sure.

HOT. Roguery I'm sure.

BELL. Confound you both.

HOT. And confound you both. (Bell. *turns them both out*.)

BELL. (*To a* Page) You Boy, is there any one at Door?

PA. Yes my Lord.   210

BELL. So, this Boy can answer, who is it?

PA. *Sir Courtly Nice,* My Lord.

BELL. O! these Rogues, have they made him wait all this while? introduce him quickly. He comes most seasonably to rid me of my plague, now I'm very sick of it.

> *Enter Sir* Courtly *and the* Page, *bowing to*
> *one another.*

Dear Sir *Courtly,* my Servants did not tell me who you were, that I have ignorantly made you wait, I am asham'd to see you.

Sir Co. Your Lordships most humble Servant.   220

BELL. Your very humble Servant – Page call my Sister.
Enter Aunt *and* Leonora.

Sir Co. (*Goes to Salute* Leo. Aunt *steps first*.) Madam your most –

192   brought 'em both] 1, 2   brought both 3
198   i'faith]   I'faith 1, 2, 3
221   Servant–Page]   Servant Page–call 1   Servant.–Page– 2   :
Servant,–Page 3

AU. Sir *Courtly,* your very humble Servant.

Sir Co. (*Salutes* Aunt.) Oh! your Ladyships very humble
Servant –

AU. Your most humble Servant.

Sir Co. (*To* Leo.) Now Madam, your most humble Servant.

AU. An incomparable fine Gentleman.   230

BELL. Well, Sir *Courtly,* now I've brought you thus far
o' your way to my Sisters inclinations; I'le leave you to pursue
the rest o' your journey by your self; you need no guide to
Ladies hearts.

Sir Co. Oh! your most humble Servant.

AU. No, Sir *Courtly* commands all. If my Neice does not
receive you, Sir *Courtly,* in all the obliging manner in the
World, 'tis for want of experience and understanding merit –
I'le assure you, Sir *Courtly,* I who have some little more judgment, have had a very particular value for you, Sir, from the 240
first Minute I had the honour to see you, Sir.

Sir Co. Oh! Madam, your most humble Servant.

AU. A very particular –

Sir Co. Oh! your most humble Servant.

AU. And if my Neice has not, it proceeds from her want
of Years to know Desert. And indeed all Youth is indiscreet,
I wou'd by no means advise a Gentleman of Merit, to marry
any Person, that has not some Years and experience upon
her –

BELL. [*Aside.*] She's setting up for her self I think. 250
Aunt –

AU. Nephew –   F3

BELL. Pray leave the Lovers together.

AU. Sir *Courtly,* your most humble Servant.

Sir Co. Madam, your most humble Servant.

AU. Pray, Neice, behave your self so to Sir *Courtly,* as
at least to do me right; and by all your expressions and behaviour, he may know how very particular an honour I have
for him.

240   a very particular] 1, 2   a particular 3

BELL. (*Aside.*) She has for him?   260

AU. Most particular.

BELL. Pray Aunt in particular – come with me –

AU. Very particular –

Sir Co. Oh! Madam – Madam –

BELL. Aunt –

AU. Yes Nephew – Sir *Courtly,* I am exceeding unwilling
to leave you to the Conversation of a young Lady, whose Years
I'm afraid will not afford her Wit enough to entertain so fine
a Gentleman –

Sir Co. Oh! Madam! Madam! Madam!   270

AU. But I'le return with all speed possible.

BELL. (*Aside.*) But you shall not, if I can help it –

AU. And so your very humble Servant.

Sir Co. Oh! Madam! your most humble Servant. (*Exit* Aunt
and Bel.)

LEO. (*Aside.*) Now will I manage him, humour him –
pretend to admire him – to draw him into love, laugh at him
and revenge my self on him, for plaguing me.

Sir Co. Now Madam, is the glorious opportunity come,
which my Soul has long wish'd, to express how much I admire, 280
adore –

LEO. Oh! Sir *Courtly* –

Sir Co. Extravagantly adore!

LEO. Oh! Sir *Courtly* – I cannot receive all this.

Sir Co. Oh! Madam, is there any thing on the Earth so
charming? I never saw anything so fine as your Ladyship, since
I was born.

LEO. Fye, Sir *Courtly.*

Sir Co. Never since I was born –

LEO. You'l kill me with blushing.   290

Sir Co. I speak my Soul – Heavens! what Divine Teeth
there are?

LEO. Fye! fye! I shall never open my mouth more.

Sir Co. Then you'l undoe all the World. Oh! there's nothing
so charming as admirable Teeth. If a Lady fastens upon my
heart, it must be with her Teeth.

LEO. That's a pleasant Raillery – ha! ha! ha! (*Feigns a Foolish laugh.*)

Sir Co. Oh! Madam, I hope your Ladyship has a better opinion o' my good Manners – Railly   a Lady o' your 300 quality?

LEO. Oh! you Wits, turn all things into ridicule.

Sir Co. Madam, I never was so serious since I was born; therefore I beseech your Ladyship have pitty upon me. I swear and vow if you do not, I shall dye.

LEO. Dye! ha! ha! you Wits will be raillying.

Sir Co. Heavens, Madam! how shall I convince you, I am serious?

LEO. Really, Sir *Courtly,* I shou'd be very sorry if you be serious.   310

Sir Co. Oh! Heavens! why so Madam?   F3ᵛ

LEO. Because 'tis pitty so fine a Gentleman shou'd lose all his Gallantry –

Sir Co. Now you frighten me, Madam. Is it impossible for me to attain the Glory of your inclinations?

LEO. It will be impossible for me to keep the Glory of your inclinations, Sir *Courtly;* so I dare not venture on 'em.

Sir Co. Oh! as to that, Madam, I'le swear Eternal constancy, eternal services, and all those things.   320

LEO. You are not in your own power, Sir *Courtly.* You fine Gentlemen, like fine Countries, are desir'd and sought by all, and therefore in a perpetual War. If I shou'd place my heart in you, it wou'd not have a minutes quiet. A thousand Potent Beauties wou'd every day assault you, and you'd yield out o' Complaisance, your good Breeding wou'd undo me.

Sir Co. Oh! Madam, this is extremity o' Gallantry; your Ladyship pushes things to a strange height.

LEO. I speak my Soul. Besides I've another humour, but 330 that's a *Foibless* will ridicule me.

Sir Co. Oh! Madam.

326   yield out o' Complaisance]   1, 2   yield a Complaisance   3

LEO. Nay I'le confess it. I am strangely curious – extravagantly curious – I nauseate a Perfume if it ever saluted any Nose but my own.

Sir Co. Oh! fortunate! my own humour.

LEO. Nothing must come near me, that was ever once touch'd by another.

Sir Co. Is it possible?

LEO. Not if you'd give a Hundred pound.   340

Sir Co. My own Phrase too, I've observ'd it in my self, I'me strangely fortunate – (*Aside.*) we shall be fond to an infinite degree.

LEO. For that reason, your fine Gentleman is my aversion, he's so tempted by all Ladies, so Complaisant to all Ladies, that to marry a fine Gentleman, is to accept the leavings of a Thousand Ladies.

Sir Co. Oh! Madam! you ha' met with the Creature you desire; I never touch'd Woman since I was born.

LEO. That's pleasant, I believe you have ruin'd a thousand. 350

Sir Co. Not one upon my Soul.

LEO. 'Tis impossible.

Sir Co. Oh! Madam! there's not one Lady in a thousand I can Salute. I only touch the tip o' their ear with my Cheek.

LEO. Fy! fye!

Sir. Co. Not one Lady in a Million, whose breath I can endure. But I cou'd not go into their Beds, if you'd give me a Thousand pound. I cou'd not come into the Ayr of any Bed in *England* but my own, or Your Ladyships, if you'd give me all the World.   360

LEO. This is all Gallantry, Sir *Courtly*. You have been told this is my humour.

Sir Co. Is it really, Madam?

LEO. Oh! above all things. I suffer nothing to come near my bed, but my Gentlewoman.

335 own] 3   one 1, 2
340 you'd] 1, 2   you 3
344 Gentleman]   Gentlemen 1, 2, 3
355 Fy! fye!] 1   Fye! fye! 2, 3

Sir Co. Nor I, but my Gentleman. He has a delicate hand   F4
at making a Bed, he was my Page, I bred him up to it.

Leo. To making Beds?

Sir Co. Ay, Madam, and I believe, he'l make a Bed with
any Gentleman in *England*.   370

Leo. And my Woman has a great Talent.

Sir Co. Is it possible? Ladies commonly employ ordinary
Chamber Maids – with filthy Aprons on, made by sluttish
Women that spit as they – spin – foh!

Leo. Foh!

Sir Co. Your Ladyship will pardon me — my Linnen is all
made in *Holland,* by neat Women that dip their Fingers in
Rose-water, at my charge.

Leo. Delicate.

Sir Co. And all wash'd there.   380

Leo. And so is mine at *Hearlem*.

Sir Co. At *Hearlem,* I hold a constant correspondence with
all the Eminent Washers there.

Leo. That's delicate, and agrees /wonderfully with my
humour.

Sir Co. Oh! happy! we shall be fond to an infinite degree.
Enter Surly.

Leo. Oh! foh! here's that beastly rude Clown Mr. *Surly*.

Sir Co. Oh! foh! what shall we do with him?

Sur. How now? how now? you two are intimate – heark 390
you, Madam.

Leo. Oh! foh!

Sir Co. Foh!

Sur. Foh! what's this fohing at?

Sir Co. No body Mr. *Surly;* only at present we are accosted
with an ungrateful smell.

Sur. Yes, I smell an ungrateful smell, your Rogury. Madam,
I employ'd this Fellow to speak for me, and I'le be hang'd if
he be not false to me.

Leo. To speak for him? ha! ha!   400

Sir Co. Ay, for him, Madam, ha! ha!

390   two are intimate] 1, 2   two are too intimate   3

Sur. Ay, for me Nickumpoop.

Sir Co. Your humble Servant Sir, y'are very civil.

Sur. So I am, that I do not execute thee for this theft upon the place; but thou plead'st thy Face, as Whores do their Bellys; 'tis big with Fool.

Sir Co. Very civil – Sir.

Sur. Sure, Madam, a Woman o' your sence, will not chuse him before me. He has more Land? not more improv'd Land. His Acres run up to one great Weed, I mean himself; and there   410 it Blossoms in Periwigs and Ribons. Oh! but he has a finer Person! that's a cheat; a false Creed impos'd on you, by a General Council of Taylors, Milleners and Sempstresses; let my hat expound his Face, and youl see what a peice o' simple stuff it is.

Sir Co. Horrid! he has put his beastly Hat upon my Head –   F4ᵛ
(*To a* Ser[vant].) pray Sir do me the favour to remove it, or I shall grow very sick –

Sur. Sick? I hope thou wilt eat my Hat. Now, Madam, you see what a cheat he is, and whether he deserves any more   420 favours, then to be decently hang'd with the rest of his Brothers.

Sir Co. My Brothers hang'd, Mr. *Surly*?

Sur. I mean the Pictures in the Hangings, for they and thou are all but Needle-work; and thou would'st serve for a peice o' Tapstery, but for a Husband, Lord, ha' Mercy on thee.

Sir Co. Your Servant, Mr. *Surly.* You are a very well bred Gentleman, Sir, and pay great Veneration to a Lady o' Quality, and your Mistress – ha! ha!

Leo. His Mistress? ha! ha!   430

Sir Co. Let's railly him to death, Madam – ha! ha!

Sur. Railly? does the ridiculous Figure pretend to laugh at any thing?

Sir Co. De'e hear, Madam?

Leo. Sir *Courtly,* you are a Martyr to good manners, and

405   upon the place]   1, 2   upon this place   3
426   Tapstery]   1, 2   Tapestry   3
434   De'e]   3   Dee'   1, 2

suffer out o' respect to me, more than is fit for a Man to bear.

SUR.   He a Man? I ha' seen a Butler make a better thing out of a Diaper Napkin.

Sir Co.   Your most obliged humble Servant – Sir.

LEO.   Sir *Courtly,* I'le withdraw, that you may do your self 440 Justice – (*Aside.*) and be kick'd –

Sir Co.   Your Ladyships most humble Servant.

LEO.   I'le no longer protect such a Coxcomb – (*Aside.*) as your self.

Sir Co.   Your very humble Servant, Madam; I'le push his Soul out presently.

LEO.   Oh! don't do him that favour, Sir, only correct him.

Sir Co.   Well, Madam, what your Ladyship pleases. Your Ladyships very humble Servant. (*Exit* Leo.) Mr. *Surly,* I have receiv'd some favours from you, Sir, and I desire the honour 450 of your Company, Sir, to Morrow morning at *Barn-Elms,* Sir, please to name your Weapon, Sir.

SUR.   A Squirt.

Sir. Co.   A Squirt?

SUR.   Ay, for that will go to thy heart, I'm sure.

Sir Co.   Well, Sir, I shall kiss your hands.

SUR.   Kiss my Breech.   (*Exit.*)

Sir Co.   Beast, Clown, Fool, Rascal. Pox take him – what shall I do with him? it goes against my stomach horribly to fight such a Beast. If his filthy Sword shou'd touch me, 'twould 460 make me as sick as a Dog.   (*Exit.*)

Scene a Garden. Enter Cr. *and* Leonora.

LEO.   Ha! ha! I'le secure the Coxcomb – I'le get him confin'd upon the Guard, among Tobacco takers, and that will confine him to his Bed and Bagnio's for one Month.

CR.   That will do rarely. About this time I expect Mr. *Fare-wel,* I ha' sent for your Brother to introduce him.   G

LEO.   My Brother?

CR.   Your Brother I say, to shew my skill. Retire, and stay

439   Your most obliged humble]   1, 2   Your humble obliged   3
455   to thy heart]   1, 2   to my heart   3
463   Coxcomb–I'le]   1, 3   Coxcomb–get   2

conceal'd in the Garden. Here your Brother comes. (*Exit* Leo.) 470
   Enter Belguard.
Now for lies and nonsence to entertain this jealous Brother
till the Lover comes.

   BELL. Sir *Thomas* your Servant, what's your will with me?

   CR. Talk – I love talk – begin.

   BELL. Very pithy.

   CR. In what circumstance are we?

   BELL. Circumstance?

   CR. Ay, what call you this, where we are?

   BELL. A Garden.   480

   CR. A Garden? I've seen in the *Indies* a Melon as big.

   BELL. As all this Garden?

   CR. Bigger.

   BELL. (*Aside.*) Well lyed of a Mad-man. Are all your Fruit
so large?

   CR. All.

   BELL. Your Nutmegs and Pepper are not.

   CR. Your History is erronious. We have Nutmegs as big as
small Fly-boats, I have sail'd a hundred Leagues in a Nutmeg.

   BELL. (*Aside.*) Well lyed.   490

   CR. Our Oysters have wonderful conferrence.

   BELL. Circumference I suppose you mean.

   CR. Y'ave nick'd it. Three of 'em block up a Harbour. 'Tis
our way of Mortification.

   BELL. Fortification.

   CR. You are in the right – Pox on't I have been so long
abroad, I have almost forgot my Mother tongue. (*Aside.*) Well
– when will this Lover come? 'tis near the hour, and delicately
dark.

   FARE. (*Within.*) Murder! murder! murder! (*Clashing of* 500
Swords.)

   CR. (*Aside.*) That's he! he's come! murder cryed out.

   BELL. And at my Coach-house Door?

   FARE. (*Within.*) Oh! Cowardly Rogues! Four upon one.

   BELL. A Gentleman assassinated?

497 abroad] 1, 2   aboard 3

CR. Open the Door.

BELL. Who's there?

Enter a Servant.   G^v

SER. My Lord.

BELL. Call some o' the Servants to assist a Gentleman, set 510
upon at my Coach-House Door.

CR. Ay – quick – quick –   (*Draws.*)

BELL. How, Sir *Thomas*? will you venture among 'em?

CR. De'e think I wont? a Gentleman and not fight?

BELL. I must not suffer it, you may be hurt.

CR. No Sir, I'le fight like a Gentleman; I'le come by
no hurt I'le warrant you. Come quick – quick – open the
Door.

Enter Servants.

Now Sound a Trumpet, Tivy – tivy – tan tan – tivy – 520
Tone, – Pox on't 'tis a Horn – I don't know a Horn, I ha'
forgot every thing belongs to a Gentleman – among 'em – helter
skelter – (*Exit Bel. Cr. and* Ser. *Mean while* Farewel *steals into
the Garden.*)

Enter Leonora *and her* Woman.

LEO. I' my conscience this is Cracks design to let in Mr.
Farewel.

FA. Dear Madam you are in the right.

LEO. Mr. *Farewel*? I know your voice –

FA. Oh! Madam, I adore you for this bounty.   530

LEO. And I shou'd blush for it.

FA. Why so, Madam?

LEO. Shou'd a Woman admit a Lover by night at a Back-
Door into the same house where she lyes, and converse privately
with him before Marriage?

FA. Your Brother admitted me.

LEO. 'Tis true indeed, you may thank him for the favour,
I thought your sufferings deserv'd pity, and my Brother wou'd
let me shew it, no other way.

FA. A thousand Blessings on you.   540

514 De'e] 3   Dee' 1, 2
534 where] 2, 3   wher 1

LEO. I doubt not but my honour is very safe in your keeping, I wish your Person, were as secure in mine.

FA. I am glad o' the danger, since tis some assurance o' my Love.

LEO. Your Friend Mr. *Crack* plays his part very well, and I doubt not but he will secure us here, and conveigh us hence, but then other dangers will follow you.

FA. What are those, Madam?

LEO. The danger of marrying without a Fortune, my Ten thousand pound is at my Brothers dispose.   G2

550

FA. I am glad of that too, Madam, 'twill shew my love is not mercenary.

LEO. The danger of being laught at by the Wits, for marrying at all.

FA. Oh! let the Wits keep the Jilting rotten Wenches, and leave the sweet Virtuous Ladies to us marrying Fools, I can be as well pleas'd to keep a fine Wife to my self, as they can be to maintain fine Wenches for all the Town.

LEO. Nay, your keeping Men, Keepers like have commonly but the Offals for their Slave. Well the Evening Ayr will 560 be unwholsome to you, if you stay longer in it, you'l be in danger of Thunder and Lightning presently, I mean my Brother – he comes – follow me – (*Ex.* Leo. Fa. Wom.)

Enter Belguard, Crack, *&c.*

CR. What Cowardly Rogues were these? they ran upon our first sallying.

BELL. They had a reason, you'r a *Lyon*.

CR. I us'd to kill *Lyons* and *Tygers* in the *Indies,* as you do *Hares* and *Conyes* here. I kept a *Tyger* Warren, I kill'd a brace every morning to get me a stomack.   570

BELL. It was a good one sure, you offer'd dear for it. Well I hope you ha' got no hurt?

CR. Yes, something very sharp, went quite through my stomack.

551   shew my love]   1, 2   shew that my love   3
557   fine]   2   five   1, 3
560   Slave]   1, 3   Slavery   2   :   Share M. Summers

BELL. How? through your stomack? then you cannot live.

CR. Yes, if you noint it presently with a good dish o' Jelly-broth, and Tent it with a bone o' Roast-beef.

BELL. Is that the wound? it shall be heal'd presently.

CR. Presently, for my stomack is Captious.

BELL. It shall be done. [*To* Servant.] Go to my *Aunt* and   580
desire her to order Sir *Thomas* his Supper –

SER. She's not very well, my Lord, and gone to bed.

BELL. Then let the Steward do it. Sir *Thomas* I am going
out and shall stay late. Pray command my house – good Night
to you –   (*Exit.*)

CR. Your Servant Sir – you keep a Woman? now to the
Lovers – where are they?

Enter Farewel, Leo. *and her* Woman.

FA. Here! here! thou Divine Fellow.

CR. So, so, kiss! kiss! kiss!   590

LEO. Before Marriage?

CR. Ay, for fear you shou'd not kiss after marriage – well
the house is our own, and the Night our own – your *Aunts*
gone to bed, and your Brother abroad, we'l Tory-rory, and
'tis – a fine Night, we'l Revel in the Garden – Slaves go bring
my Supper – quick – quick –

     Ex. Slaves — *and enter with Dishes*: Farewel,   G2ᵛ
        Leo. *and* Crack *sit down.*

Enter Siamites *and* Bantammers.

Now a Song and Dance o' your own fashion – but shut the   600
Garden-Gates – and look to 'em well, for I'le be private in my
pleasures – (*A Song and* Indian *Dance.*) So – now to my
Chamber – well – there is no publick Officer like your Pimp.

    Pimps manage the great business o' the Nation.
    That is – the Heavenly work o' propagation.
                        (*Exeunt Omnes.*)

593   *Aunts* gone] 1, 2   *Aunt* goes   3
594   Tory-rory] 1, 2   Tory-tory   3

Scene Cracks *Chamber. Enter* Farewel *and* Crack.

FA. Oh! thou Divine Fellow, what joys hast thou pro-
cured me?

CR. What joys?

FA. All that Innocence cou'd afford.

CR. Innocence? that's insipid stuff.

FA. No Mr. *Crack,* there's difference between the *Mannah*
that came, from Heaven, and that out of 'Pothecaries Shops;
a touch of *Leonora's* hand like *Mannah* from Heaven has all
that Man can fancy. Here she comes.   10

Enter Leonora.

This, Madam, is bountiful after an Evenings Conversation,
to afford me a Morning too.

LEO. We shou'd be charitable to Prisoners.

FA. I am a Prisoner, but such a happy one, as a King
is when Lodg'd in a Royal Tower, to prepare for his Coronation. My hour of Coronation draws near, I want only the
Church Ceremony and the Oath.

CR. Madam, how dirst you venture hither, by day light?

LEO. My Aunt, and Brother, are both gone abroad, and 20
won't come home till Noon. So all those hours are mine, and
now Mr. *Crack* to requite your Musick I ha' brought some o'
mine to entertain you.

A Song – And enter a Woman.

WOM. Oh! Madam – undone – your Brother.

CR. How? how?

WOM. Just coming up stairs, to visit – you Sir *Thomas.*

CR. Pox of his civility. Hide, Sir Hide. And do you *Women*
shreike! shreike! and cry out murder. (Cr. *throws himself on
the ground and scrambles in distracted postures after the* 30
Women. *They shreike –)*

Enter Belguard.

BELL. So, here's my Sister got into the Madman's Room;

15   I am a Prisoner] 1, 2   I am Prisoner 3

and has put him into a frantick fit. Oh! the insatiable curiosity
o' Women.

CR. You Whores! you bewitching Whores, do you come
to bewitch me? I'le fetch blood from you.

BELL. Why wou'd you offer to come hither, Sister?

CR. What are you, Sir, the King of *Bantam*?

BELL. No Sir, no.   40 G3ᵛ

CR. Oh! the *Mogul.*

BELL. Nor the *Mogul.*

CR. What do you then with all these Concubines? Oh! I
know you now, you'r a fine man, you have put me into brave
circumstances. Did not I desire you to let me see no Women?
and here, you keep a company o' rambling Whores in your
house, that have put me into the circumstances o' distraction.
I was a top o' the Staircase taking a prospect o' the Cape of
Good-Hope, and these Flyboats came sayling under my Nose.
What do me I? but leap down to break their Necks? and ha' 50
broke my own I think. I am certain, I have broke something,
but what I don't know. Pray take me up, and look over my
bones, see if none be missing; if they be, Bone for Bone will
be demanded.

BELL. Poor creature! who's there?

CR. Who's there? will you trust me to your servants! so
if a Leg or an Arm of mine be broke, they'l leave it behind
'em, and I shall loose it. I expect all my Limbs and Bones
from you, as you received 'em. So – come and take account
of 'em.   60

BELL. I will – I will –   (*Takes him up.*)

CR. Oh! have a care – Oh!

BELL. Alas! I fear he's hurt; your foolish curiosity has done
this? did you not gape enough upon him before?

CR. Oh! gently! gently! so – so (Bell. *leads him out.*)

FA. Oh! this pleasant Rogue! ha! ha!

LEO. Tis an excellent fellow. As soon as we hear my

57 behind 'em] 1   behind e'm 2   : behind them 3
63 has] h'as 1, 2   : ha' 3
64 upon him before?] 1, 2   before upon him? 3

Brother is returning, slip into that passage, 'twill lead you to *Crack's* Bed-chamber.

Enter Aunt.   70

Au. How now Gentlewoman? a man wi' you? Nephew – Nephew – Nephew.

Leo. Begone – begone – through that Entry.

Ex. Fa. *at one Door, at another Enter* Bellguard.

Bell. What's the matter?

Au. Our family's dishonour'd, dishonour'd – here was a fellow, a handsome young fellow wi' my Neice. Oh! my flesh! my flesh.

Leo. Wi' me?

Au. Will you deny it Confidence?   80

Bell. Who's there? *Hothead, Testimony,* all of you come hither.

Enter Hothead, Testimony.

Test. What's your honours pleasure?

Bell. To cut all your throats, you are all Bauds and   **G4**
Villains.

Hot. Leave me out o' the number you had best.

Bell. I will not Sir, For here was a young fellow wi' my Sister.

Leo. My *Aunt's* whimsy and jealousie.   90

Au. I cou'd tread you under my feet.

Bell. Which way went he?

Au. Into that passage: He cannot be got further, then Sir *Thomas Calicoes* Bed-chamber.

Bell. Lock all the doors, Arm and beset Sir *Thomas Calicoes* lodgings.

Leo. This will prove such another wise business as the Picture.

Bell. Hold your peace – get you into that room wi' my *Aunt. Aunt* pray look to her. (*Ex.* Bell. Hot. Test. &c.)   100

---

69 *Crack's*] 2   *Crak's* 1 : *Cracks* 3
83 *Enter* Hothead, Testimony.] 2   *Enter* Hothead, Testimony, *Exit.* 1, 3

Au. I'le keep her, I warrant her – come in gentlewoman
– you are a fine gentlewoman.

Leo. (*Aside.*) Oh! my heart trembles – Heaven inspire
Crack.

> *Ex.* Aunt *and* Leonora. *Scene changes to another*
> *Room. Enter* Farewell *and* Crack.

Fa. Oh! cursed fortune.

Cr. Well don't trouble your self. I'le bring you off safe.

Fa. Not trouble my self, when *Leonora's* honour is in
danger? she'l be the jest of every prating Fop, and malitious 110
beauty.

Cr. Her honour shall be safe too. This blustering – Brother
shall entertain you.

Fa. With a Blunderbuss?

Cr. Ay, full o' Claret. Away – away – he comes.

> *Ex.* Fa. *and Enter* Bellguard, Hothead, Testimony,
> *and the* Servants *arm'd.*

Cr. How? the High and glorious Emperour o' *Siam* with
all his guards? Thou most invincible *Paducco, Farucco, nel-*
mocadin – bobbekin – bow – wow – wow – why dost thou 120
seek to destroy us *English,* seated on thy Dominions by thy
own Letters Patents?

Bell. Pish! take him away.

Cr. Take away our Priviledges? then this goes to my heart.

> *Draws his Dagger, and pretends to stab himself.*

Bell. Hold, hold – Sir *Thomas* – Sir *Thomas,* no hurt is
ment to you.

Cr. Most Great and Glorious Emperour, I humbly thank,
and do humbly Impore thee; that thou wou'dst command thy 130
Invincible guards, to lay down their arms, and put us out of
our frights, and we'l submit our persons to thee. (*Aside.*) This
is some Interlopers work.

Bell. Pox o' this impertinent mad – coxcombe! Lay down

your wea / pons, may be if we humour him, he may come to   G4ᵛ
his sences, and give us leave to search the rooms. (*They lay
down their Weapons*).

Cʀ. My Lord *Bellguard,* your most humble servant.

Bᴇʟʟ. He's come to himself; that's well. Sir *Thomas* your
servant, how do you?   140

Cʀ. A little discompos'd, something has frightned me, and
put me into the circumstance of a sweat.

Bᴇʟʟ. I'me sorry for that. Shall I beg leave, to search your
rooms for a theif that's got in?

Cʀ. Pardon's beg'd; search must not be made; for I have
a friend there, you must not see.

Bᴇʟʟ. (*Aside.*) Wou'd you and your friend were hanged.

Cʀ. A very honest Gentleman, but very much addicted to
marriage. 'Tis he that I told you, is to marry my Indian Fubs
of a Sister – Mr. *Farewel.*   150

Bᴇʟʟ. Mr. *Farewel*?

Cʀ. Ay, hearing of my arrival, and what circumstance I
was in, hover'd all this morning about the house to get a sight
o' me; but car'd not to come in, for it seems there is enmity
between you.

Bᴇʟʟ. 'Tis True, and I wonder how he got in without my
knowledge.

Cʀ. I made him come in. I was throwing my legs about
in the Hall, and the door being open, our eyes knock'd immediately, and gave remembrance such a bang, that we ran full 160
speed into the circumstances of embracing.

Bᴇʟʟ. And pray who saw this?

Cʀ. Who saw? what care I who saw? I care not if the whole
Town saw, I'm not asham'd of owning Mr. *Farewel.*

Bᴇʟʟ. No Sir, but I mean which of my family saw? that I
may thank 'em for their care.

---

141   frightned]   1, 3   frighted   2
147   see. Wou'd. . .hanged. (*aside.*)]   1, 3   see. *Bell.* Wou'd. . .hang'd.
(Aside.)   2
161   embracing.]   embracing?   1, 2, 3
166   'em]   3   'm   1, 2

CR. What do I care for your family? if I may not bring a
friend into your family, a fart for your family.

BELL. Nay be not angry Sir *Thomas,* your friend's wel-
come.   170

CR. I doubt it not, for I have found you a very civil person.
And now recollection is active, I fancy he's the man you take
for a theif. Tis so – ha! ha! – excuse me – ha! ha! – leave is
implord – ha! ha! brother *Farewel.*

FA. (*Within.*) Brother.

CR. Come out, and participate o' laughter.

BELL. [*Aside.*] So, now have I play'd the fool again, vex'd
my self, and wrong'd my Sister with my impertinent jealousies.

Enter Farewel.

CR. Come brother – ha! ha! laugh – but first salute.   180

FA. My Lord, I believe you wonder to see me here, and you
may; I call my self Bastard, and renounce the blood o' my
family, by coming under your roof with any design, but to
prejudice you, which at present I must acknowledge to my
shame is not my intention. I visit my friend here for his / own   H
sake, and the sake of a great Beauty, which you shall not
hinder me of, My Lord.

BELL. I will not Mr. *Farewel,* I scorn those effeminate
revenges. If I hurt any Man it shall be with my Sword.

FA. Your Sword, my Lord?   190

CR. Hold! hold.

BELL. Ay any where but here Mr. *Farewel,* my House is
your Sanctuary, and here to offer you violence, wou'd prejudice my self.

CR. What a quarrelling's here? i' my conscience I believe,
My Lord, 'tis because you think he came to steal me, I being
under whimsical circumstances, for I remember you call'd him
a Thief. Look you, My Lord don't fear me, I won't be stole –
I know when I'm well – Brother I'm very well provided for,
I want nothing but my Wits; and what do they signifie? if a 200

191   Hold! hold.]   Hold? hold.   1, 2, 3
196   steal me]   1, 2   steal to me   3
199   very well]   1, 2   well   3

Man lives like a Gentleman, no matter whether he has Wit or no –

FA. Well, my Lord, though I have the misfortune to be your Enemy, I am none to good manners; I am sorry I ha' given your house this trouble, and the more because my Friend receives such generous usage in it.

BELL. Nor am I an Enemy to Love, and the fair Sex. If the Lady you come for loves you, for her sake I wish you success.

FA. Now my Lord you vanquish me.

CR. He's a brave Man – Faith.   210

FA. I fancy we shall live to be better Friends, at present I'le take my leave, my Lord your Servant.

BELL. Your Servant Sir.

CR. Brother I must see you down stairs. This was a Master-peice. Ha! ha!   (*Exit* Fa. *and* Cr.)

BELL. Now I am cool again. What a flame had your negli-gence put me into. (*To a* Servant.) Here release my Sister, I'm asham'd to see her –

HOT. Sirrah! Sirrah! you did this to make me suspected.

TEST. Ay – ay, I must be abus'd, because I'm a Protestant. 220

HOT. A Protestant? a Dog. But with such Names the Rogues divide the Rabble, and make the Nation go like the Devil, upon Cloven Feet.

BELL. Hold your prating, and by your future care make amends for your past negligence; your trouble shall not be long, within this Eight and forty hours I'le marry her, or send her into the Country.

HOT. Well – well – I'le look to her, for the Honour of my Family, not your huffing.   (*Exit.*)

TEST. I to discharge a Conscience –   (*Exit.*) 230
Enter Leonora.

LEO. So – Sir –

BELL. My Sister –

LEO. Do you run from me? is that the reparation you make

201   lives like a] 1   lives a   2, 3
229   not your] 1, 2   no your   3

for the intolerable wrongs you have done me? (*Pretends to burst into tears.*)

BELL. Well, I have wrong'd you, I'm sorry for it, and beg your Pardon – / I must be gone – about business – your business – to fetch Sir *Courtly Nice*. Your Servant, Sister.   H^v

LEO. Oh! your Servant Sir – ha! ha! – he runs – I may 240 chance Sir to run as nimbly from you, if *Cracks* Wit do not fail him – here he comes –

Enter Crack.

Thou admirable Fellow, what has thou done with Mr. *Farewel*?

CR. He's in the Street staying for you.

LEO. Staying for me? and can'st thou conveigh me to him?

CR. De'e question it? put on a Vizard and something over your Cloaths.

LEO. Sweet Rogue.

CR. Nay, nay be gone.   250

LEO. Delicate Rogue.

CR. Nay, nay he stays for you.

LEO. Incomparable Rogue.

CR. Pshaw! put on your Vizard.

LEO. Most excellent Rogue.

CR. Oones! put on your Vizard.

LEO. I will – I will – ha! ha! toll – loll – derol –

    Cr. *goes out, and as* Leo. *is going out singing and danceing, She's met by* Bell. *and* Sir Co.

BELL. Oh! Sister your tune's alter'd.   260

Sir Co. Oh! Madam! I'm happy to find your Ladyship, in so gay a humour.

LEO. (*Aside.*) You'l not find it so –

BELL. Sir *Courtly* I'le betray her to you. I left her in Tears upon an unhappy occasion, and at parting told her I wou'd bring you. Now you are come, I find her in joy. Nothing else cou'd cause the change.

Sir Co. Oh! fortunate.

LEO. (*Aside.*) Oh! Fop!

BELL. Now improve your interest, and let us see how 270

247 De'e] 2, 3   Dee' 1

great a Master you are in Courtship, by your dextrous dis-
patch. I leave you together –   (*Ex.*)

Sir Co.   And upon my Soul I will. Oh! Madam, am I so
Fortunate, so Glorious, to be well in your fine inclinations?

Leo.   Oh! fye, Sir *Courtly* – if I had any such guilt upon
me, do you think I wou'd confess?

Sir Co.   You do confess, Madam – your fine Eyes, and
your languishing Ayr, and your charming Blushes, and all those
things –

Leo.   I hope I carry no such false things about me; for if   280
they say any such thing they infinitely wrong me.

Sir Co.   Oh! now you are cruel, Madam; you kill me.

Leo.   Can you hope for my heart Sir *Courtly,* till I've some
assurance o' yours.

Sir Co.   What assurance wou'd your Ladyship have?

Leo.   All manner – he that pretends to my heart – must
sigh, and wait, / and watch – and pant – and fight, and write   H2
– and kill himself.

Sir Co.   All this I ha' done, Madam, and Ten thousand
things more. Drove by your Windows, a thousand times a day,   290
sought you at the Parks and the Plays. Was a constant faithful Attendant at all Tragedys – for I presum'd your Ladyship
nauseates Comedys –

Leo.   Oh! Foh!

Sir Co.   They are so ill-bred – and sawcy with Quality,
and always cram'd with our odious Sex – that have not always
the most inviting smell – Madam, you'l Pardon me – Now at
Tragedies, the House is all lin'd with Beauty, and then a
Gentleman may endure it. And I have gone, found not your
Ladyship there, drove home, kill'd my self with sighing, and   300
then writ a Song.

Leo.   Oh! Heavens! Sir *Courtly,* did you ever write a Song
upon me?

Sir Co.   Above a thousand.

Leo.   Oh! there's nothing charms me like a Song – For
Heavens sake – the Song! the Song –

300   sighing] 2, 3   sigthing   1

Sir Co. I've above forty here in a sweet Bag, I'le shew
you the first I made upon Your Ladiship. 'Tis thought to be
a pretty Foolish soft Song, most Ladies are very kind to it.

> As I gaz'd unaware,   310
> On a Face so fair;

Leo. Oh! Sir *Courtly* –

Sir Co.   Your cruel Eye,
> Lay watching by
> To snap my heart,
> Which you did wi' such art;
> That away wi't you ran,
> Whil'st I look'd on.
> To my ruin and grief;
> Stop Thief – stop Thief.   320

Leo. Oh! fine! oh! fine!

Sir Co. That stop Thief, Madam, is pretty Novel.

Leo. Oh! delicate! I'm charm'd! I'm lost! fye what have
I said –

Sir Co. What makes me the happyest of Creatures.

Leo. I only railly – I renounce all –

Sir Co. Not for the World –

Leo. Away – the Song again – the Song – I'le hear nothing
but the Song. Is there no tune to it?

Sir Co. One of my own composing.   330

Leo. That accomplishment too? Heavens! how fine a
Gentleman is this?

Sir Co. Oh! Madam, how proud you make me?

Leo. Oh! dear, how I betray my self? foolish Creature –
no more – no more – the Tune, the tune.

Sir Co. I always humour my words with my Ayr. So I
make the Voice shake at the last Line, in imitation of a Man
that runs after a Thief. (*Sings.*) Sto – ho – ho – hop – Thief –

Leo. Oh! delicate! cannot I learn it? sto – ho – ho – ha!   H2ᵛ
ha! ha! (*Imitates his Foolish singing and falls into a laugh.*) 340

317 That] 1, 2   Than 3
331 too] 3   to 1, 2

Sir Co. Dear Madam, what makes your Ladyship laugh?

LEO. At a Coxcomb, that thought to win me with a Foolish Song, this puts it into my head.

Sir Co. Oh! Foolish! there are abundance of those Foolish Fellows, and does the Song please your Ladyship?

LEO. Infinitely, I did not think you had been so fine a Poet.

Sir Co. Poetry, Madam, is my great foible, and when I see a fine Woman I cannot command my foible.

LEO. How? de'e make Songs upon other Ladies? unfortunate – I've given my heart to an inconstant Man –   350

Sir Co. Oh! Madam, only Gallantry.

LEO. I'm abus'd – unfortunate – (*Pretends to weep.*)

Sir Co. Oh! Madam, you take it wrong –

LEO. I'm abus'd.

Sir Co. Oh! Heavens!

LEO. But the Songs very fine! sto – ho – ho – ha! ha! (*Sings and laughs.*)

Sir Co. Pleasant Creature.

LEO. (*Aside.*) Coxcomb.

Sir Co. We shall be infinitely fond – (*Looks in a Glass.*) 360 a pretty Glass, this Madam.

LEO. (*Aside.*) So he's making an assignation with his own foolish Face, I'le leave him to Court that and steal away. (*Exit.*)

Sir Co. Sto – ho – ho – hop –

Enter Aunt.

AU. Singing, Sir Courtly?

Sir Co. (*Looks in the Glass while he speaks.*) At your Service, Madam. Well, Madam, you have said so many fine things to me, that I assure my self of your heart, and now I am resolv'd to push this opportunity, to an extremity o' 370 happyness.

AU. (*Aside.*) Oh! fortunate! this to me? I did make him some advances to day I confess, and have they had this suc-

349   de'e]   2, 3   dee'   1
       unfortunate–]   2   unfortunate I've   1   :   unfortunate, I've   3
367   *in the Glass*]   1, 2   *into the Glass*   3
369   my self]   1, 2   your self   3

cess? my heart pants: I am surpris'd with infinite joy, and am
not able to answer –

Sir Co. Well, Madam, I must be happy, and so upon my –
the Lady gone –   (*Turns from the Glass.*)

Au. Sir *Courtly* you put me in great confusion –

Sir Co. (*Aside.*) The Lady's consent is very considerable –
she governs her Neice, and under her conduct may make me 380
happy, with a reserve to Modesty. Well, Madam, shall I have
your consent to my happyness, my glory?

Au. Oh! dear Sir! is it possible to answer you so soon?

Sir Co. So soon, Madam? you know my passion has been
long.

Au. Is it possible? I swear I never heard of it before.

Sir Co. That's strange; wou'd not my Lord, your Nephew
acquaint you?

Au. He never said one word of it to me.

Sir Co. That's amazing.   390
                                                      H3
Au. (*Aside.*) I find my Nephew has been false to me.
It seems 'tis me the Gentleman loves, and my Nephew wou'd
defraud me of him, for his Sister – heres fine doings.

Sir Co. I swear I thought your Ladyship had known, and
granted your consent – you said so many fine things –

Au. I said no more, Sir *Courtly*, then what were the result
o' my thoughts, upon the contemplation of your great desert –

Sir Co. Your Ladyships most humble Servant – then I
hope, Madam, since my passion has been long, though you
knew not of it, you will not deferr my hapyness – 'tis in 400
your power I'm certain, no Person controuls you –

Au. Controuls me? that's pleasant – no Sir.

Sir Co. (*Aside.*) She says true – she can bring her Neice –
I beseech you, Madam, take pity of a suffering Lover.

Au. Oh! Sir, shou'd I consent so soon, 'twou'd be against
all Forms.

Sir Co. I would not for the World offend against any
Forms. No Man living more studyes, and adores all manner of
Forms – but my passion has been long.

Au. I know not what to say, Sir, indeed I must not.   410

Sir Co. Oh! Pardon me!

Au. Oh! Pardon me!

Sir Co. Oh! Madam!

Au. You confound me, Sir.

Sir Co. You distract me, Madam. It must be –

Au. Well, Sir I yield, but with an extremity o' blushing.

Sir Co. Your most obliged humble Servant.

Au. My severe temper wou'd never ha' been wrought on so soon, but by so fine a Gentleman.

Sir Co. Your most humble Servant.   420

Au. And to revenge my self on my Nephew, for his false play.

Sir Co. Well, Madam, we'l in my Coach to the next Church presently.

Au. 'Tis very hard to resist you, Sir *Courtly*. If you please I will first put on a Disguise; for I desire it may be manag'd with all secrecy, till the Ceremony of Marriage be over.

Sir Co. With all my Soul; for I infinitely love a secret Intrigue, especially when every body knows of it.

Au. Least my Nephew light on us, and prevent it.   430

Sir Co. He's for the Match.

Au. He's very false.

Sir Co. Is it possible?

Au. Is it not apparent, when he conceal'd the whole matter from me, least I shou'd promote it?

Sir Co. That's unanswerable, I'm amaz'd at it. Well, Madam, I shall not fail of being happy?

Au. Immediately, Sir.

Sir Co. And you think you have power?

Au. Power? that's pleasant.   440

Sir Co. (*Aside.*) So – so – she'l bring or send her – Well, Madam, Your most humble Servant.

Au. Your very blushing Servant –   (*Ex.*)   H3ᵛ

Sir Co. Your humble – sto – ho – ho – hop – Thief – (*Exit.*)

436   unanswerable] 2, 3   unanswreable 1

Enter Crack *and* Leonora *laughing.*

CR. A humble Thief indeed, steal an old Woman?

LEO. This was a pleasure I cou'd not ha' thought of. Now
to our Affair.

CR. Come – on with your Vizard.   (*Exeunt.*) 450
        Scene changes to the Hall. Enter at one
        Door, Hothead *and* Testimony, *at*
                another Crack.

CR. Barbarity! falsehood! treachery! murder!

HOT. What's the matter?

CR. Did not I stipulate upon the surrendry of my self
to this House, to be kept from Women? and I am devour'd
with 'em; here's come into my Chamber, a hot burnt Whore,
with a black crust upon her face – here she is, Avant.
(*Exit.*)   460
        Crack *pulls in* Leonora *vizarded.*

HOT. You damn'd Whore, how came you into this house?
and what are you? I'le see your face.

CR. Then I'le see your braines, I swear by Gogmagog,
and all the seven damnable Sinnes.

TEST. Oh! sad! oh! sad!

CR. Shew me the face of a Woman? I had rather see forty
full moons.

HOT. Stand off Impertinence; I will see her face.

CR. Murder! murder! call my Lord – Lord, Lord – murder 470
– murder! Lord – Lord – Lord.

HOT. Hold your bauling, I'le let her go. For now I think
on't, If my Lord shou'd find this Whore here when he gave
such strickt orders, we shou'd let no body out, or in, he'l make
more noise than this mad fool – so let us kick her out o' Doors,
and say nothing.

TEST. Hold, let us not use violence to her – (*Aside.*) she's
a great temptation to me. I'le reprove the idle Woman, it may
be, I may gain upon her.

```
454  murder!]    murder  1  :  murder.  2, 3
458  'em]   3     e'm   1, 2
461  pulls]  3     pull's  1, 2
```

Hot.   Gain a Clap Sirrah! for this is some of the footmens   480
Whores, pick'd up in the dark. Get you out you Whore.

Test.   No violence pray. (*Aside.*) She's a great snare to me.
Woman get you out woman – and de'e hear? I'le follow you,
and we'l drink a bottle.

Leo.   Do old godly knave, and thou shalt be welcome.

Test.   (*Aside.*) I come! I come! get you out woman.

Hot.   Get you out – you Whore. (*They thrust* Leo. *out.*)

Cr.   Good morrow – up so early?

Hot.   What's the whimsy now?

Cr.   Am not I i' Bed?   490 H4

Hot.   In Bed?

Test.   Poor soul, poor soul –

Cr.   I am not i' faith. Then I walk in my sleep: I was fast
a sleep just now, and dream't I saw women, and Vizards, and
all that Trash; and the fright put me in a Feaver. I burn;
prethee give me a mouth full of sweet ayr.   (*Exit* Cr.)

Hot.   Prethee take a belly full and be damn'd. A fine time
on't I have; with Whores, and Fools, and mad Men, and
Fanatiques.   (*Exit.*)

Test.   So, now I'le steal after her, for I find in me a very   500
great uproar.   (*Exit.*)

           Scene changes to Violante's *house. Enter*
           Farewel – Leonora *vizarded,* Testimony.

Fa.   Come in, come in honest old Fornicator, though the girle
be mine, when I have had my collation, if she'l consent, faith,
thou shalt have a bit; I love a Wenching Rogue i' my heart.

Test.   Oh! dear Sir, your very humble servant, and truly I
am a kind of a wag. I love a pretty bit sometimes.

Fa.   And I love thee the better for it, and this is a pretty bit,
thou shalt see her. (Leo. *pulls off her vizard.*)   510

Test.   Oh! dear! undone! undone!

Leo.   Nay, nay Mr. *Testimony* won't you be as good as
your word? shan't we have a Bottle?

---

483   de'e]   3   dee   1, 2
504   come in honest]   1, 2   come honest   3
510   *pulls*]   *pul's*   1, 2   :   *pull's*   3

TEST. Oh! Madam, don't discover me to my Lord, and you shall not only have my prayers, but the prayers of all the sober party for you all days o' my life.

LEO. So, he runs from Whoring to Praying.

FA. Are not you a Rogue Sirrah?

TEST. I know I shall be called Rogue, by the *Popish* party – they will rejoyce at my fall, but I hope my fall will be sancti- 520 fied unto me for my better Upstanding.

FA. Among the Wenches – Sirrah – come, Sirrah, you shall stay till my Lord comes, for his mortification, as well as yours.

TEST. Oh! my flesh, it has undone me.

Enter Violante, *and* Crack.

VIO. My dear.

LEO. My dear.

VIO. Excellent *Crack;* for this great peice o' service, I'le ha' thee knighted under a petticote. Well we must send for my 530 Lord, to laugh at him.

TEST. Oh! dear! I tremble!

VIO. Who's there? tell my Lord, I desire to speak with him.

LEO. Pray let him bring Sir *Courtly Nice,* and his bride with him; be sure you say nothing o' me. (*Ex.* footm.)

VIO. Are you a Bride yet?   H4v

LEO. Not yet.

VIO. Get in, and let my Chaplain make you one.

LEO. Come Mr. *Testimony*. Mr. *Crack,* bring him.

CR. How now you Rogue? what's your business?   540

TEST. Oh! my reproach will be great (*Ex.* Fa. Leo. Cr. Test.)

VIO. Mr. *Surly*.

Enter Surly.

SUR. Well, what now?

VIO. Now, you shall be my Husband.

SUR. Your Jack, to turn and roast you for another, whilst I ha' no share in you.

533 tell] 2   well 1, 3

VIO. According to the share I have in you: You men wou'd feign engross all manner o' Sinnes, by the pretended Prerog- 550 ative o' your Sex; well if iniquity be your Estate, when you ha' married me, I'le put in for my thirds.

SUR. I doubt it not; within this week, I shall see in a Fop's hand, a *Billet Doux,* that is a Ticket to let him into your Play-house.

VIO. Prethee leave off this doged humour.

SUR. I ha' none; fawning is a Dogs humour.

VIO. Nay but Sullenness; it taxes thy Estate, that thou art never the better for it; tis a french Estate.

SUR. Ay, but to lick a fool's shoe, is a Spaniel's Estate.   560

VIO. Prethee dress like a Gentleman.

SUR. So I do; but I wou'd not dress like a Gentleboy, lag at my years among those Children, to play with their Toys; be always followed up like a love letter, with a superscription, these to the next pretty girle.

VIO. There's no altering thee – go in a while.

> *Ex.* Surly. *Enter Lord* Belguard, *Sir* Courtly,
>
> Aunt *vizarded.*

VIO. My Lord, your humble servant. I invited you hither, to reconcile you to your Sister, she's weary of your Govern- 570 ment, and has dispos'd of her self.

BELL. Ay, Madam, but according to my own desires, that now I suppose you will acknowledge the good effects of my Government; Sister salute your friend.

VIO. Do you take that for your Sister? then I'le shew you the good effects of your Government. Open the Door.

> *The Scene is drawn, and* Farewel, Leonora,
>
> *a* Parson, Crack, Testimony, *appear.*

BELL. My Sister there? call my servants.

CR. Nay then call mine, the great *Mogul,* and the King 580 o' *Bantam,* I'le pepper you.

BELL. Then you were the Pimp were you – Sirrah – I may chance begin with you.

556   off]   of   1, 2, 3
564   followed]   1   folded   2, 3

VIO. How? i' my House and presence? touch him if you   I
dare.

BELL. I'm made an Ass on.

CR. Not far from that circumstance.

BELL. You Rascal –

VIO. Again?

Sir Co. But what the Devil am I made? what have I got? 590

LEO. Even my stale *Aunt*.

AU. Sawcy huzzy.

Sir Co. The *Aunt*? what have you put upon me, Madam?

AU. What have I put upon you, Sir, more than your self
desir'd? Did not you declare you have long had a passion
for me?

Sir Co. A Passion for you? Comical! that's probable! Rot
me if ever I had a Passion for you in my Life. I meant all to
your Neice; a Passion for an old Woman?

AU. Ill-bred Fop.   600

Sir Co. Very fine –

VIO. Now, my Lord, what say you of your fine Cotqueen
art of Conserving Woman? will she keep if not candied with
Virtue? here is a peice o' dryed Sweetmeat, you see cou'd not
keep; and proves by her example, that the Huffs of either Sex,
when they are boldly attacqued in private, soonest deliver their
Weapons.

AU. This is all ill manners.

VIO. Ay, but here's an old Cat will suffer no Vermin to
come into the House; but then he has a Liquorish tooth, and 610
loves to have a sweet bit for himself; he wou'd fain ha' pick'd
up your Sister for a Wench.

BELL. How?

TEST. 'Tis true indeed my Lord; I will not tell a lye for the
whole World.

BELL. Oh! Villain – well Sirrah – I'le leave you to my Cousin *Hotheads* correction.

VIO But your faults my Lord I'le take into my correction,
and give my self to Mr. *Surly* – Mr. *Surly*.

          Enter Surly.   620

SUR. Well –

BELL. To *Surly*?

SUR. Ay, now *Nice* thy quarrel and mine is at an end, I'le let thee be an Ass forty years longer.

Sir Co. You are a rude fellow and you are all ill-bred – and I'le revenge my self on you all, as far as my Sword and my Wit can go –

LEO. Wit – ha! ha!   (*All laugh.*)

Sir Co. Very fine manners this – my Coach – (*To the Aunt.*) Madam, you may follow your own occasions – I have 630 none with an Old Woman.

AU. You are a Coxcomb.

Sir Co. Your Servant – my Coach –

LEO. Must I lose you Sir *Courtly* – stop Theif – stop Theif –   I

Sir Co. Oh! your Servant – my Coach you Dogs – (*Ex.*)

VIO. Come my Lord, I see Patience in your Face, all may be well yet.

SUR. How! Jilting already?

VIO. Promise I shall enjoy all and singular the Priviledges, Liberties, and immunities of an *English* wife.   640

BELL. All.

VIO. That is to say, Ramble, Rant, Game, Dress, Visit, Prate, Ogle, Kiss – and –

BELL. Hold – hold – whether the Devil is she running: Kiss, kiss – and – stop for Heavens sake.

VIO. Kiss, and before your Face; is it not the Prerogative of an *English* Wife? *Surly*, I owe thee a reward for Service, kiss me.

BELL. That's not to be borne.

VIO. *Surly*, I am thy Wife.

BELL. Hold – hold – for Heavens sake – do not use me 650 thus!

VIO. Then do not Rebel but practise obediently, the postures of an *English* Husband, before you are Listed; Poise your Hat, draw your left Leg backward, bow with your Body, and look like an Ass, whilest I kiss like a – Wife – *Surly* kiss me.

BELL. If he does –   (*Lays his Hand on his Sword.*)

625 are all ill-bred–] 1, 3   are ill-bred– 2

SUR. With all my Heart. If I kiss thee, let the Devil Marry thee. (*He offers to kiss her, and she gives him a box o' th' Ear.*)

VIO. And the Devil kiss thee, cou'dst thou think any Wo- 660
man wou'd suffer thy face to come near her, but some Dairy Maid, to curdle her Milk?

ALL. Ha! ha! ha!   (*All laugh.*)

SUR. Hoh! hoh! What a society o' Gotam's are here, to laugh at a Man for missing a Woman? had I Married her, as my Lord *Wise-acre* intends to do, I had deserv'd to ha' been laught at, for a Coxcomb, and a Cuckold, as he wiil be in few Days.

VIO. How?

SUR. Ay, you are all Whores, Pox on you, all Whores. (*Ex.*) 670
        Enter Hothead *and all the* Servants.

HOT. Did you send for us?

BELL. Yes, do you see where my Sister is?

HOT. By what witchcraft was this?

VIO. Do not you remember a Vizard you turn'd out o' Doors?

HOT. Was it you?

LEO. Even the same.

HOT. Then you deserve to be turn'd out o' Doors again.

BELL. But what do you deserve Sir? that not only turn'd my 680
Sister out o' Doors – but let Mr. *Testimony* – pick her up for a Wench.

HOT. Oh! Dog – oh! Rogue –

TES. I am no Rogue – a Man may fail, and be Godly in the   I2
main – I am satisfied in my Spirit, I am a Godly Man –

HOT. Here's a Rogue – Sirrah – Sirrah – (*Beats and kicks* Tes.)

TES. Persecution – Persecution – *Papist* – do – kick the Godly, kick the Protestants out o' Kingdom – do *Papist* – I see what you wou'd be at –   (*Ex.*) 690

662   Maid] 2, 3   Milk   1
665   at a Man] 2   at Man   1, 3
675   Do not you] 1, 2   Do you not   3
689   out o' Kingdom] 1, 3   out o' th' Kingdom   2

BELL.   So Cousin now I have done with spyes – you may follow your own business, if you have any –

HOT.   Business? yes I have business, and will have business as long as there is a *Fanatick* in the Kingdom, and so farewell –   (*Ex.*)

BELL.   I am now convinced, Vertue is a Womans only guard. If she be base Metal, to think by Chimistry, to turn her into Gold,

> *Is a vain dream of what we never see,*
> *And I'le proclaim to all – It cannot be.*   700
>
> > (*Exeunt Omnes.*)

FINIS.

A SONG to be Sung in Dialogue between a Man and a Woman in the Third Act, to Sir *Courtly Nice,* at his first appearance.

MAN.   Oh! be kind, my Dear, be kind,
             Whilst our Loves and we are Young.
         We shall find, we shall find
         Time will change the Face or Mind;
             Both will not continue long.
         Oh! be kind, my Dear, be kind.

WOMAN.   No, I Love, and fear to loose you,
         Therefore 'tis I must refuse you,
             When I've yielded you my Crown
             You'l no more Obedience own.   10
         No, I Love, and fear to loose you.
         Therefore 'tis I must refuse you.

MAN.   The Fair by kindness Reign,
             By cruelty Destroy.
         If you can Charme with the Pain
             Of Love, then what can you do
                 with the Joy?

694   a *Fanatick*]   1, 2   any *Fanatick*   3
696   Vertue is]   3   Vertue a   1 : Virtue is   2

         The Fair by kindness Reign,
              By cruelty Destroy
WOMAN.   I fear to yield, but cannot deny.   20
MAN.   If you do not I shall die.
WOMAN.   So shall I.
BOTH.   So shall I.
CHORUS. Then come to Joy – come to Joy,
         Better Love than we shou'd die.
         Come to Joy, come to Joy.

                    A Song.   I2ᵛ

A Dialogue Sung between an *Indian* Man and Woman, in the
Fourth Act, to *Farewel, Violante, Crack*. Being an imitation of
a Song, Sung by some Natives of *India,* before the late King.

MAN.   *Thou lovely* Indian *Sea of Charms.*
            I'd envy no Jaw-waw *alive*
            Might I be so blest to dive
            In thy soft yielding Arms
         With a Jimminy, Gomminy, whee-whee, whee.
         With a Gomminy, Jimminy-whee.
WOMAN. *I wou'd if you'd be true,*
            But when you've done
            You'l be gone,
            And throw me off with a Shooh-shooh, shooh.   10
            And a hush pooh,
            And a fush whooh,
         And a migotty, magotty, migotty, magotty,
            Migotty, magotty, shooh.
MAN.   *No, no, my other Females all*
            Yellow, Fair or Black,
         To thy Charmes shall prostrate fall,
            As every kind of Elephant *does*
            To the White Elephant *Buitenacke.*

  3   *so blest*] 3   *so, blest* 1, 2
  5   a Jimminy] 1, 3   with Jimminy 2
 10   *off*] 3   *of* 1, 2

And thou alone shall have from me   20
    Jimminy, Gomminy, whee, whee, whee,
    The Gomminy Jimminy, whee.

WOMAN. *The great* Jaw-waw *that Rules our Land,*
    And pearly Indian *Sea*
    Has not so absolute Command,
    As thou hast over me.
    With a Jimminy Gomminy, Gomminy
    Jimminy, Jimminy Gomminy, whee.

BOTH. *Thou alone shalt have from me*
    Jimminy Gomminy, Gomminy,   30
    Jimminy, Jimminy Gomminy,
    Whee, whee, whee, whee, whee, whee.

Epilogue.   A4

'Tis a hard Case, an Audience now to please,
For every Pallat's spoyl'd with some Disease.
Poor Plays as fast as Women now decay,
They'r seldom car'd for after the first day;
How often have I heard true wit call'd stuff,
By Men with nothing in their Brains but Snuff?
Each Shante Spark, that can the Fashion hit, ⎫
Place his Hat thus, role full Forsooths a Wit; ⎬
And thinks his Cloaths allows him judge of it. ⎭
The City Gallant, the *Exchange* being done,   ⎫   10
Takes Sword at *Temple-Bar* which Nice stuck on. ⎬
Comes here and passes for a *Beaugarzoon.*   ⎭
Audacious Vizards too, so fast do grow,
You hardly can the Virtuous from 'em know.
Nay Parents now not only can endure,
Their Childrens faults, but what is worse procure.
Of Old the Mother full of Parent sway,

   8   role full,]   3   role full   1, 2
  15   not only]   1b   not likely   1, 2, 3
  16   what]   1, 2, 3   which 1b
  17   the Mother]   1, 2, 3   Proud Mother   1b

Kept Miss a Vassal to her work all day;
And to the Wooing Spark Miss was not brought,
But some fine Golden thing her wheedle wrought: 20
Now you shall meet young Lady and her Mother,
Rambling in Hackny-Coaches masqu't together;
Yes, and to say the truth, to work they go,
Fine work but – such as they will never shew.
Unless some Nott to draw a Fool to Wed,
And then he finds Miss rare at work a Bed.
But the Grand Randevouz is kept of late,
Exact at Nine, hard by o're *Chocolate*.
Sad fate, that all the Christian Youth o' th'Nation,   A4ᵛ
Should be oblig'd to *Jews* for Procreation.   30
Nay, what is worse, that's, if reports be true,
Many a Christian Gallant there turns *Jew*;
That is, so oft some rotten Strumpet plyes him,
The Chirurgion's forc't at last to Circumcise him.
Our *Bridges-street* is grown a Strumpet Fair,
Where higling Bawds do Palmb their rotten Ware.
There *Fowler* like the watching Gallant Pores
Behind his Glove, to get a shot at Whores;
And from his tongue lets flye such charming Words,
That strait he carrys off the wounded Birds.   40
Another waits above in the great Room,
Till a new Cargozoon of Strumpets come.
There by three Glasses plac't the Affected Dunce,
Acts you Four *Courtly-Nices* all at once;
Our Gallerys too, were finely us'd of late,
Where roosting Masques sat cackling for a Mate:
They came not to see Plays but act their own,

20   wheedle]   1, 2, 3   Needle   1b
23   say]   1, 2, 3   Speak   1b
25   Nott]   1, 2, 3   Net   1b
28   *Chocolate*]   1b, 2, 3   *Chocholate*   1
37   the watching]   1, 2, 3   a watching   1b
40   strait he carrys off]   1, 3   off he carries streight   1b   :   strait
he carries off   2
45   Gallerys too,]   1, 2, 3   Galleries were   1b

And had throng'd Audiences when we had none.
Our Plays it was impossible to hear,
The honest Country Men were forc't to swear: 50
Confound you, give your bawdy prating o'er,
Or Zounds, I'le fling you i' the Pitt, you bawling
    Whore –
This Comedy throws all that lewdness down,
For Virtuous Liberty it pleads alone:
Promotes the Stage to th' ends at first design'd,
As well to profit, as delight the Mind.

APPENDIX A

THE / PROLOGUE / AND / EPILOGUE / To the New /
COMEDY, / Called, / Sir Courtly Nice, or, / It Cannot be. /

The Prologue.

What are the Charms by which these happy Isles,
Have gain'd Heavens brightest, and Eternal Smiles?
What Nation upon Earth besides our own,
But by a loss like ours had been undone?
Ten Ages scarce such Royal worth display,
As England Lost, and Found, in one strange day.
One hour in Sorrow and Confusion hurl'd,
And yet the next the Envy of the World.
Nay, we are Blest in Spite of us, 'tis known,
Heavens Choice for us, was better than our own.   10
To stop the Blessings that o'reflow this day,
What heaps of Rogues we pil'd up in the way?
We chose fit Tools against all good to strive,
The Sawciest, Lewdest Protestants alive.
They wou'd have form'd a Blessed Church indeed,

51 o'er] 3   o're 1, 2
54 that] 1, 2, 3   this 1b
55 it pleads] 1b   is pleas'd 1, 2, 3
57 As well to profit, as] 1, 2, 3   At once to Profit and 1b

Upon a Turn-Coat Doctors Lying Creed;
To know if e're he took Degree is hard,
'Tis thought he'l have one in the *Palace-Yard.*
Plot-Swallowers sure, will Drink no more Stuff down,
From that foul Pitcher, when his Ears are gone.   20
Let us Rely on Conscience, not on Cheats,
On Heavens Wisdom, not State-Juglers Feats.
How greatly Heaven has our loss supplyed?
'Tis no small Vertue Heals a Wound so wide:
Nay, in so little time to Rear our Head,
To our own Wonder, and our Neighbours dread.
They see that Valour Crown'd with Regal Power,
They have oft seen with Lawrels Crown'd before.
Verse is too Narrow for so great a Name;
Far sounding Seas hourly repeat his Fame.   30
Our Neighbours Vanquish'd Fleets oft wafted o're,
His Name to theirs, and many a Trembling Shore.
And we may go by his great Conduct Lead,
As far in Fame as our Fore-Fathers did.
At Home, he milder ways to Glory chose;
God-like, by Patience, he subdued his Foes:
Now they, and their Designs are Ruin'd all,
Beneath their fallen accurst Excluding Wall:
These are not all the Blessings of this Isle,
Heaven on our Nation in a Queen doth Smile,   40
Whose Vertues, Grac'd by Beauty, shine so bright,
All the Fair Sex to Vertue she'l Invite,
And all our Clouds turn to a Glorious day,
By this Illustrious pairs United Ray,
Who both Reform and Grace us by their Sway.

The Epilogue.

To plead for Freedome in so free a time,
May seem Impertinent, if not a Crime.
The Circling Sea, gives Limits to our Shores,
But nothing bounds our Rabble, Wives, or Whores.

In Spite of all Indulgent Sway can do. 50
Our Croud, their Lust of Faction will persue,
And either Sex will to their Joys go on,
Scorning all ills to Honour, Purse, or Bone.
Nay, Parents now, not only can endure
Their Childrens Faults, but which is worse, procure,
Of Old, Proud Mother, full of Parent Sway,
Kept Miss a Vassal to her work all day;
And to the Wooing Spark, Miss was not brought,
But some fine Golden thing, her Needle wrought.
Now you shall meet Young Lady and her Mother, 60
Rambling in *Hackney-Coaches,* Masqu'd together.
Yes, and to Speak the Truth, to work they go,
Fine work, but such as they will never show;
Except some Net to draw a Fool to Wed,
And then he finds Miss rare at work – a Bed.
Nay, we have gotten other Schools of late,
As *Masquerades,* and the *Jews Chocolate.*
There Fowler like, a watching Gallant pores,
Behind his Glove, to get a Shot at Whores,
Whose Coach and Bones comes Ratling to the Dores. 70
Nearer he creeps, discharges some kind words,
And off he carries streight the wounded Birds.
Another Gallant waits in the great Room,
Till a New Cargazon of Strumpets come;
And there with his own Face he Treats his Eyes;
What need he see, he can Act Comedies?
There by four Glasses plac'd, as for the nonce,
Sir Sparkish Acts four Coxcombs all at once.
Our Galleries were finely us'd of late,
Where Roosting Masques sate Cackling for a Mate; 80
They came not to see Plays, but Act their own,
And had throng'd Audiences when we had none:
Both Pit and Gallery was a Strumpet Fair,
Where Higling Whores, Sold Rotten Pumpions dear.
This Comedy throws all this Leudness down,
For Vertuous Liberty it pleads alone;

Promotes the Stage to th'ends at first design'd,
At once to Profit and Delight the Mind.

LONDON, *Printed for* Tho. Benskin *at the Corner Shop in*
Little-Lincolns-Inn-Fields. 1685.

APPENDIX B
A Calendar of Performances

1685	4 May		DL	United Company
	11 May		DL	
	9 November		Court	
1686	10 May		DL	
	20 October		Court	
	3 November		Court	
1689	31 May			
1690	30 April		Court	
1703		(Doran)	Bath	
	21 September		LIF	"Never acted there before"
	30 October		DL	
1704	4 February		LIF	
	24 October		DL	
1705	5 January		DL	
	3 March		DL	
	27 July		LIF	
	17 October		DL	
	17 December		DL	
1706	22 November		Queen's	
1707	17 January		Queen's	
	23 October		Queen's	
1708	2 February		DL	
	5 October		DL	
1709	4 February		DL	
	6 October		Queen's	

	21 December		Queen's
1710	28 June		Greenwich "A new Prologue"
	7 September		Greenwich
	16 November		Queen's
1711	26 May		DL
	26 November		DL
1712	12 December		DL
1713	24 March		DL
	July-August		Oxford
	23 October		DL
1714	2 April		DL
1715	29 January		DL
	22 March		DL
	19 October		DL
1716	16 January		DL
	19 January		DL
	11 April		DL
	27 April		DL
	9 June		DL
	29 November		DL
1717	25 February	(Rosenfeld)	Norwich
	1 March		DL
	16 May		DL
	3 October		DL
1718	3 January		DL
	6 June		DL "By Royal Com-[mand]"
	6 October		Hampton Court
	7 October		DL
	29 December		DL
1719	22 April		DL "By His Majes-ty's Command"
	15 September		DL
	27 November		DL
1720	13 October		DL
	30 November		DL

1721	11 May		DL	
	7 November		DL	
1722	31 January		DL	
	11 May		DL	
	20 October		DL	
1723	3 January		DL	
	16 May		DL	
	24 October		DL	"By Command"
	20 November		DL	
1724	10 January		DL	
	20 January		New Haymarket	
	5 February		New Haymarket	
	24 October		DL	
	4 December		DL	
1725	20 March		DL	
	21 September		DL	
	31 December		DL	
1726	11 February		DL	
	25 May		DL	
	1 October		DL	
1727	4 January		DL	
	7 March		DL	
	19 May		DL	
	21 November		DL	
1728	29 November		DL	
1729	6 March		DL	
1734-35		(Lowe)		
1735-36		(Lowe)		
1739	summer	(Rosenfeld)	Canterbury	London Company
1741	summer	(Rosenfeld)	Canterbury	
1746	14 April	(Summers)	DL	
	9 August		Richmond Hill	
1747	June	(Rosenfeld)	Ipswich	Norwich Company
1748-49		(Nicoll)	CG	

1751	17 October	(MacMillan)	DL	"Not acted five years"
	18 October	(MacMillan)	DL	
1753	6 November	(MacMillan)	DL	
	14 December	(MacMillan)	DL	
1758	6 July	(Summers)	CG	*Sir Thomas Callicoe*
	24 November	(MacMillan)	DL	
1759	24 April	(Pedicord)	CG	
	15 May	(Pedicord)	CG	
1764	27 March	(Summers)	CG	"Not Acted 4 years"
1770	25 April	(Summers)	CG	
1781	28 April	(Summers)	CG	

III. EXPLANATORY NOTES

A. NOTES TO CHAPTER I

1. *Stage History*

(Unless otherwise indicated, information concerning performance dates and acting casts in this section and in Appendix B is taken from lists supplied by Emmett L. Avery. This material was later included in his volume (Part II, 1700-1729) of *The London Stage, 1660-1800,* published 1960-62.)

P. 22. *Theatre Royal.*

The second Theatre Royal at the corner of Bridges Street and Drury Lane was designed by Christopher Wren and opened March 26, 1674.

P. 24. *Covent Garden.*

Designed by Edward Shepherd, Covent Garden theatre opened December 12, 1732, under the management of John Rich, who moved to it the troupe from the old theatre in Lincoln's Inn Fields. After Rich's death in 1761 Covent Garden passed to Bancroft and Beard, and between 1767 and 1777 was owned by George Colman and three others.

P. 24. *Trial of the actors.*

Powell, Mills, Wilks, Mrs. Verbruggen, Mrs. Oldfield, Johnson, Pinkethman, Bullock, Griffin, Cibber, and Jane Rogers were accused of having acted "obscene, profane, and pernicious comedies" (*Volpone, Sir Courtly Nice,* and Thomas Baker's *The Humour of the Age*) at Drury Lane between June 24, 1700, and February 24, 1701. The jury found only Pinkethman guilty.

Pp. 24-25. *Role of Sir Courtly Nice.*

Mountfort, William (c. 1664-1692)	1685; 1690 (Borgman)
Cibber, Colley (1671-1757)	1703, 1706-13, 1716-25, 1727-29; 1734-36 (Lowe)
Foote, Samuel (1720-1777)	1746 (Summers); 1753 (Lowe)
Powell, George (1658?-1714)	1703, 1710
Peterson, Joseph	1740's (Rosenfeld)
Woodward, Henry (1714-1777)	1751 (MacMillan); 1764, 1770 (Summers)
Lewis, William (1748?-1811)	1781 (Summers)

Mountfort was an extremely popular actor and a fair playwright, whose death in a fight with Lord Mohun and Captain Richard Hill over Mrs. Bracegirdle was a scandal of the time and a favorite topic for dramatic historians and biographers then and now. For a full account of this, and of his association with Justice Jeffreys, see Albert Borgman, *The Life and Death of William Mountfort*. Of Mountfort's unsuccessful first play Langbaine (p. 378) remarked:

"There are some *Surlyes,* who think that in this Play, Sir *Courtly writ for his Diversion, but never regarded Wit."*

Borgman also quotes Matthew Prior's *Satire upon the Poets* in regard to Mountfort's presumption as a poet and man of affairs:

> Were *Shakespear's* self to live again, he'd ne'er
> Deg'nerate to a Poet from a Player.
> Now *Carlisle* in the new-rais'd Troop we see,
> And chattering *Mountfort* in the Chancery;
> *Mountfort* how fit for Politicks and Law,
> That play'd so well Sir *Courtly* and *Jack Daw.*

Samuel Foote, the famous mimic whom Samuel Johnson threatened with public castigation if he should dare to caricature the Doctor, was, in his early years, an actor of foppish and "fine gentleman" roles.

The least known of the actors in the role was the last recorded, William Thomas "Gentleman" Lewis, who became deputy manager of Covent Garden theatre in 1782, and was described as "gay, fluttering, hare-brained Lewis".

P. 25. *Role of Crack.*

Leigh, Anthony (d. 1692)	1685
Estcourt, Richard (1668-1712)	1704
Bowen, William (1666-1718)	1706-07
Leigh, John (1689-1726)	1708
Pinkethman, William (d. 1725)	1708-13, 1717-22

Williams, [Charles]	1724
Miller, Josias (1684-1738)	1724-25, 1727
Yates, Richard (1706?-1796)	1751
Shuter, Edward (1728?-1776)	1764; 1770 (Summers)

Tony Leigh's "great role" was that of the Spanish Friar in Dryden's play of that name; the Earl of Dorset had his portrait painted in this character by Sir Godfrey Kneller. His other roles in Crowne's comedies included those of Bartoline in *City Politiques* and Stately in *The English Frier.*

Like Estcourt, John Leigh was born in Ireland, played at Smock Alley Theatre in Dublin, and tried his hand at playwriting. Recruited for the new theatre in Lincoln's Inn Fields, he played there on opening night, December 18, 1714, as Plume in Farquhar's *The Recruiting Officer.*

According to the Preface to *The English Frier* (ed. Maidment and Logan), "Bowen, who succeeded Lacy in eccentric comedy, offended at being told that Johnson acted Jacomo in the "Libertine" better than he did, sent for Quin, who had been of the party, to a tavern, drew upon him, and despite all remonstrance, pressed so furiously upon him, that Quin being compelled to draw in his own defence, so wounded him that he died within three days. For this, Quin was tried but honourably acquitted. This happened in 1718." Two of his comic roles were Teague in Farquhar's *The Twin Rivals* and Lady Pinchgut's Coachman in Crowne's *The English Frier.*

The same source indicates that Williams was "a good actor, but too fond of his bottle". He probably retired from the stage about the same time as Kynaston – around 1700. He played Young Ranter in *The English Frier.*

Miller played Teague in a revival of Howard's *The Committee,* Jeremy in *Love for Love,* and Sir Mannerly Shallow in Crowne's *The Countrey Wit,* and had outstanding success as Foigard and Abel Drugger. He is the Joe Miller of the famous jest-book, reprinted throughout the eighteenth and nineteenth centuries, but, according to the *D.N.B.,* there is no historical justification for the use of his name in the title *Joe Miller's Jests.*

Pinkethman was called by Charles Gildon "the Flower of *Bartholomew*-Fair, and the Idol of the Rabble". (*A Comparison Between the Two Stages,* 1702, p. 199). John Downes characterized him as "the darling of *Fortunatus,* he has gain'd more in Theatres, Fairs in Twelve Years, than those that have tugg'd at the Oar of Acting these 50" (*Roscius Anglicanus,* 1708, p. 52).

Richard Yates, likened by Dibdin to Underhill, was a Shakespearean clown. He played low comedy parts in many Restoration revivals in an unusually long career which ended only ten years before his death during "a fit of rage at being unable to obtain eels for dinner". (*D.N.B.*)

P. 27. *Role of Surly.*

Griffin, Philip	1685
Verbruggen, John (d. 1707?)	1706
Keene, Theophilus (d. 1719)	1707-08, 1710-13
Estcourt, Richard	1709
Thurmond, [John] Sr. (d. 1726?)	1710, 1717-18, 1720-21
Bickerstaff, John	1717, 1719
Harper, John (d. 1742)	1724-25, 1727
Berry, [Edward?]	1758

Verbruggen married Susanna, the widow of William Mountfort. Under the stage name of Alexander, he was the original Termagant in *The Squire of Alsatia,* and acted Sharper in *The Old Bachelor* and Careless in *The Double Dealer.*

Harper, the best known of the foregoing actors, was called by Davies a "lusty fat man" who played Falstaff, Ursula the Pig Woman, and other parts in low comedy and ballad opera.

John Thurmond the elder was a partner at Smock Alley Theatre, Dublin, and later played at Lincoln's Inn Fields.

Edward Berry was a Drury Lane actor who, as the King in *The Mourning Bride* in 1758, "rumbled him out in a most disgusting manner". (*Dramatic Censor* II, 413)

P. 27. *Role of Hothead.*

Underhill, Cave (1634-1710?)	1685
Johnson, Benjamin (1665?-1742)	(Downes)
Bullock, William (1657?-1740?)	1706-13
Leigh, John	1710
Miller, Josias	1717-22
Thomas	1724
Williams, [Charles]	1724-25
Shepard, Charles	1726
Woodward, Henry	1753
Bransby	1758
Quick, John (1748-1831)	1781 (Summers)

According to Downes, Johnson's first original part was that of Sir William Wisewou'd in Cibber's *Love's Last Shift* (1695/96). He played Smuggler in *The Constant Couple* and Balderdash and Alderman in *The Twin Rivals*; his performances as Morose, Corbaccio, and Hothead won the praise of Downes.

Shepard is mentioned as Sassafras in Mountfort's *Greenwich Park* in performances given in 1708, 1730, and 1735.

Quick succeeded to the parts of Shuter and Woodward after their deaths in 1776 and 1777. He excelled in old men's roles and was the favorite actor of George III.

P. 27. *Role of Testimony.*

Gillow, Thomas	1685
Norris, Henry (1665-1730?)	1706, 1710
Johnson, Benjamin	1707-13, 1717-22, 1724-25, 1727
Alleyn	1724
Taswell	1741 (Rosenfeld); 1758
Dunstall, John	1770 (Summers)

P. 28. *Role of Aunt.*

Leigh, Elizabeth	1685, 1706
Powell, Mrs.	1707-12
Baker, Mrs. Catherine	1723, 1727
Cross, Mrs.	1758

In the tradition of Mrs. Leigh's portrayal of lovesick aunts and spinsters was her performance of Lady Pinch-gut in Crowne's *The English Frier.*

Mrs. Powell played the Aunt in Mountfort's *Greenwich Park* (1708) and Lady Faddle in a revival of Crowne's *The Countrey Wit,* presented the same year.

Mrs. Baker's name appears in an agreement to act for Swiney for three years, at a salary of £40 in nine installments, dated September 9, 1709. (Nicoll, *Early Eighteenth Century Drama,* p. 286.)

P. 28. *Role of Belguard.*

Kynaston, Edward (1640?-1706)	1685
Mills, John (d. 1736)	1706-12, 1717-22
Cory, John (fl. 1700-1731)	1710
Milward, William (1702-1742?)	1724
Watson, [John?]	1724-25
Blakes, [Charles?]	1758

Kynaston in his youth acted female parts. He was the jealous Valentine in Wycherley's *Love in a Wood* (1672) and Lord Wiseman in Crowne's *The English Frier.*

Mills took the part of Merry in Crowne's *The Countrey Wit.*

Cory, an actor whose name was sometimes spelled Corey or Corye, wrote a comedy "somewhat of the Congreve style", *A Cure for*

Jealousie (1699), and later a farce taken from Molière, *The Metamorphosis* (1704).

P. 28. *Role of Leonora.*

Barry, Elizabeth (1658-1713)	1685
Verbruggen, Elizabeth (1667?-1703)	(Cibber)
Oldfield, Anne (1683-1730)	1703 (Cibber); 1706-09, 1711-12, 1718-19
Kent, Mrs.	1710
Porter, Mrs. Mary (d. 1765)	1710, 1713, 1717-19
Thurmond, Mrs. (fl. 1715-1737)	1720-22, 1724-25, 1727
Herold, Mrs.	1724
Clive, Katherine (1711-1785)	1746 (Summers); 1751
Mattocks, Mrs. Isabella (1746-1826)	1781 (Summers)

Mrs. Verbruggen was a talented comic actress and the model for Mrs. Oldfield, to whom she relinquished her role as Leonora in *Sir Courtly Nice* shortly before her death in 1703. Cibber praises her more highly than any other actress, and Gildon refers to her as "a miracle".

Mrs. Porter was discovered when very young by Mrs. Barry and Mrs. Bracegirdle, as she acted at Bartholomew Fair. She became Mrs. Barry's successor, and played many tragic roles. Samuel Johnson wrote that "Mrs. Porter in the vehemence of rage, and Mrs. Clive in the sprightliness of humour, I have never seen equalled". Her last appearance on the stage was in 1743.

Mrs. Thurmond married John Thurmond the younger, a dancer, in Dublin, and is believed to have begun her career at Smock Alley, where his father was a partner.

Mrs. Mattocks was a well-known actress of the later eighteenth century who played numerous parts in revivals of Restoration plays – among them Sylvia in *The Recruiting Officer,* Narcissa in *Love's Last Shift,* Hoyden, and Angelica in *The Constant Couple.*

2. *Sources*

P. 29, l. 8. *Comparison of Crowne with Etherege.*

A little-known critical observation upon this point has been discovered by R. G. Noyes in a work entitled *Genuine Letters from a Gentleman to a Young Lady His Pupil,* "written Some Years Since, and Now First Revised and Published, with Notes and Illustrations. By Thomas Hull, of the Theatre-Royal, in Covent-Garden. London, 1772." Thomas Hull, an actor, was probably the editor; authorship of the letters is attributed by the *British Museum Catalogue* to John

Preston, teacher. The novel is educational in purpose, and its letters, according to a reviewer "breathe a strain of the purest morality . . . . They open the understanding, and improve the taste." (*The Monthly Review,* XLVII (1772), 218.) The gentleman-tutor, Mr. Preston, writes literary letters and analyses of the classics to Miss Nancy Blisset. Letter LX, dated from Oxford, March 17, 1742/43, reviews first *Sir Fopling Flutter* and then *Sir Courtly Nice*:

The other Play, *Sir Courtly Nice,* seems to be an Imitation of *The Man of Mode,* though a faint one. Notwithstanding there are some good Things in the former, yet the Characters are not by far so genteel, nor is there so much Wit or good Sense in the Dialogue, as in the latter. *Farewel* is a sort of *Dorimant,* only not vicious. *The Aunt* is a Copy of *Lady Woodvill,* and *Leonora* of *Harriet.* The Contrast between *Hothead* and *Testimony* is diverting, but I cannot think they are naturally brought in. *Sir Courtly Nice* is well drawn, but not so delightful a Fop as *Sir Fopling*; nor do I think his Foppery savours so much of the "Gentleman." I do not know what to make of *Lord Belguard.* I think him in the main a silly Fellow, though perhaps with some Smattering of good Sense and Breeding. *Hothead's* Behaviour to him is quite *outrée, Crack's* Character appears overdone, and the unravelling of the Plot not entirely natural. *Surly* altogether is too gross, though some Part of what he says is entertaining enough. There are certainly many worse Plays. The Purpose and Tendency of this Piece being rather good than otherwise, gives it, in my Opinion, one material Ascendancy over *The Man of Mode.* (pp. 275-76.)

B. NOTES TO CHAPTER II

1. *Title Page*

P. 55, l. 10. *H.H. Jun.*

The printer of *Sir Courtly Nice* was the son of Henry Hills, Sr., the King's Printer. After 1689, when his father, a Roman Catholic, died in exile in St. Omer, the son dropped the "junior" from his name and initials. Before his death in 1713 he had gained notoriety as a pirate of poems and sermons.

P. 55, l. 10. *R. Bently.*

Richard Bentley was a bookseller at Post House in Russell Street, Covent Garden, from 1675-97. Nicknamed "Novel" Bentley, he was a well-known publisher of novels and romances, and also published Dryden's *Religio Laici* (1683) and Evelyn's *Sylva.*

P. 55, l. 11.   *Jos. Hindmarsh.*

Joseph Hindmarsh, publisher of works by Buckingham and D'Urfey, had also published anti-Catholic and Puritan works. At the Sessions at the Old Bailey on April 13, 1680, he was accused of publishing *The Presbyterians' Paternoster and Ten Commandments*. In the same year he issued Oldham's *Satyrs upon the Jesuits*.

2. *The Epistle Dedicatory*

P. 57, l. 1.   *Duke of Ormond.*

Crowne's patron, James Butler, first Duke of Ormonde (1610-1688), belonged to the illustrious family of Theobald Butler, who became hereditary butler of Ireland under Prince (later King) John. A supporter of Charles I, and a commander of Royalist cavalry, Butler was sent back to Ireland in 1641 to suppress rebellion, but was later defeated by Cromwell's forces and exiled to France. He returned to England with the king's party, and in 1661 was created Duke of Ormonde in the Irish peerage. As governor of Ireland he encouraged native commerce and learning, but his integrity made him unpopular with Charles II's courtiers. His chief enemy, Buckingham, obtained his dismissal in 1669. The next year an attempt was made on his life which stirred public sympathy in Ireland, and he was reappointed governor in 1677. He was loyal to James, although he refused to re-enter the Catholic church, from which he had become a convert to Protestantism. Upon his death he was buried in Westminster Abbey.

P. 57, l. 9.   *my Masque.*

Calisto; or, The Chaste Nymph, 1675. Montague Summers (*Restoration Comedies*, p. 395) says that Dryden, the poet laureate, was "passed over . . . through the influence of Rochester" on this occasion. Leading parts in the masque were taken by Princess Mary and Princess Anne.

P. 58, ll. 53-54.   *the latter of Confusion.*

A reference to the violence of the Whig opposition, which diminished somewhat toward the end of Charles's reign, and to the resentment created among the courtiers by Ormonde's righteous conduct.

P. 59, l. 62.   *Earl of Ossery.*

Thomas Butler, Earl of Ossory (1634-1680), was the eldest son of James, first Duke of Ormonde, and a friend of Evelyn the diarist. Ossory took up his father's quarrel with Buckingham. He participated in the naval battle against the Dutch in 1665, became rear-admiral in

1673, was nominated shortly before his death to the governorship of Tangier, an appointment he felt an unworthy reward for his own and his father's services to the king.

P. 59, l. 68. *Earl of Arran.*

The first editor of Evelyn's *Diary*, William Bray, in 1818 identified the Earl as "Richard, the younger brother of Thomas ... created an Irish peer in 1662, by the titles of Baron Butler, Viscount Tullough, and Earl of Arran; and ... an English Peer in 1673, by the title of Baron Butler of Weston. He also was deputy for his father, and distinguished himself both by sea and land, particularly in the naval engagement with the Dutch, in 1673, and against the mutinous garrison of Carrickfergus. He died in 1685."

P. 59, l. 76. *Young Earl of Ossery.*

James Butler, second Duke of Ormonde (1665-1745), was the second but eldest surviving son of Thomas, Earl of Ossory. Although a Tory, Ormonde ("Ossory") did not like James II and gained favor with William III. He became lord-lieutenant of Ireland, in which capacity he presented Swift with the deanery of St. Patrick. As a result of participation in a Jacobite enterprise, he was exiled in France and Spain after 1715, and his estates were confiscated. After the death of his brother Charles, Earl of Arran, in 1758, the titles of the family became extinct.

3. *The Prologue*

P. 61, l. 6. *As England lost ... Day.*

On February 6, 1685, Charles II died and was succeeded by his brother James II.

P. 61, l. 11. *To stop the blessings ....*

A reference to the Exclusion Bill, which would have kept the Duke of York from the throne. It resulted from anti-Catholic feeling aroused by the Popish Plot and was passed by Commons, but rejected by the Lords, before the dissolution of Parliament in January, 1681.

P. 61, l. 14. *The sawciest, lewdest Protestants alive ....*

The Whigs, under the leadership of Shaftesbury.

P. 61, l. 16. *Turn-coate Doctor.*

Titus Oates (1649-1705), the inventor of the "Popish Plot", was the son of an Anabaptist preacher who had served as a chaplain during the Civil War but had been dismissed by General Monk in 1654 for "stirring up sedition in the army". The father, Samuel Oates, re-entered the Established Church and received the living of All Saints, Hastings, in 1666, but was expelled in 1674 for "improper practices". Titus Oates was enrolled at Merchant Taylors' School in 1665 but was expelled during his first year. He studied at Cambridge but left in disgrace, nevertheless managing to become ordained. He served as his father's curate until, as the result of a scandal, he was imprisoned and his father ejected from his living. Oates escaped from prison, went to sea, and was expelled from the navy. He then turned to the betrayal of Catholics to the government for profit. He went so far as to enter the Roman Church, and studied at two seminaries, from both of which he was dismissed. After his exposé of the "Popish Plot" he enjoyed a period of popularity with Protestant zealots, but was later tried for perjury before Jeffreys and given a heavy sentence. At the accession of William III he was released, joined the Baptists, but was expelled in 1701 as a "disorderly person and a hypocrite". (*D.N.B.*)

P. 61, l. 17. *Degree.*

Oates claimed a doctorate of divinity from Salamanca, but had apparently only enrolled in 1677 at a Jesuit college in Valladolid, from which he was expelled for "scandalous behavior." He entered a seminary at St. Omer, from which he was also expelled. Of his earlier career at St. John's College, Cambridge, his tutor, Dr. Thomas Watson, wrote, "He was a great dunce, ran into debt; and, being sent away for want of money, never took a degree." Cf. Dryden, *Absalom and Achitophel*, ll. 657-659:

> The spirit caught him up, the Lord knows where;
> And gave him his rabbinical degree,
> Unknown to foreign university.

P. 61, l. 18. *Palace Yard.*

The area before the north entrance to Westminster Hall where public executions and other punishments took place. Here Titus Oates was pilloried May 18, 1685.

P. 61, l. 20. *when his Ears are gone.*

In actuality, Oates's penalty consisted of paying a heavy fine, being unfrocked, standing in the pillory annually on a specified date, and being whipped on May 20, 1685, from Aldgate to Newgate, and on May 22 from Newgate to Tyburn. His sentence to life imprisonment was commuted at the accession of William III.

P. 61, l. 28. *with Lawrels Crown'd.*

These and the lines following refer to James's reputation as a naval hero. As Duke of York he had been appointed Lord High Admiral of England before he was five years old and had acquired a reputation for personal bravery as a soldier in Continental wars during his exile. At the Restoration James was in command of the fleet, and later maintained his interest in the navy, although he was probably not personally responsible for the naval reforms with which he is credited. In the Second Dutch War a sea victory under James won him a brief period of adulation, and in the Third Dutch War many Englishmen believed that he would have obtained victory if he had been supported by the French.

P. 62, l. 31. *Our Neighbours vanquish'd Fleets.*

A reference to the defeat of the Dutch navy in the Second and Third Dutch Wars. Peace in each case was costly to the English.

P. 62, l. 35. *At home he milder ways to Glory chose.*

James's policy of moderation during the period when his succession was endangered was intended to secure toleration for Catholics as well as for dissenters. After the revelation of the "Popish Plot" the Whigs demanded the removal of James from the King's counsels and he went into exile in The Hague, from which he was recalled at the illness of Charles in 1679. James was appointed high commissioner in Scotland, where, according to Bishop Burnet, "he bore himself impartially and moderately". As reaction developed against Monmouth and the Whigs, James gained in influence over the king and returned to England in 1681.

P. 62, l. 38. *fallen, accurst, Excluding Wall.*

A reference to the failure of the Exclusion Bill and the decline in the fortunes of the Whigs. Shaftesbury had been forced to flee the country after the failure of the Rye House plot, an attempt to assassinate Charles and establish Monmouth on the throne.

P. 62, l. 40. *a Queen.*

Mary of Modena (Maria Beatrice Anne Margaret Isabel d'Este), James's second wife, whom he married in 1673. A Catholic, she was regarded by many Protestants as an agent of the Pope. After the death of James in 1701 she induced Louis XIV to recognize her son as King of England, an act which precipitated the War of the Spanish Succession.

4. *Act I*

P. 65, l. 75. *verjuice.*

A medicine or condiment made from the acid juice of sour, unripe fruit. The *N.E.D.* cites this passage as a figurative usage.

P. 65, l. 86. *Fanaticks.*

A term applied to non-conformists by members of the Established Church.

P. 66, l. 106. *Scandalum Magnatum.*

A legal offense, consisting of the "utterance or publication" of a malicious report concerning a person holding "a position of dignity". On this charge Titus Oates was arrested May 10, 1684, for calling the Duke of York a traitor.

P. 66, l. 114. *Toads. . .when they are hang'd and dryed.*

The toad, believed to be poisonous itself, was used to combat other poisons, in infections and diseases such as cancer. Also, cf. Herrick, *Hesperides,* p. 209:

> A charme, or an allay for Love
>
> If so be a Toad be laid
> In a Sheeps-skin newly flaid,
> And that ty'd to man 'twil sever
> Him and his affections ever.

P. 67, l. 134. *Tyburn.*

By metonomy, "hanging".

P. 68, l. 189. *kickshaw.*

From *quelque chose,* in the restricted meaning of a fancy dish in cookery. Cf. Shakespeare, *Henry IV,* v, i, 25:
". . . a joint of mutton, and any pretty little tine kickshaws."

P. 69, l. 208. *Bowels.*

The seat of tender and sympathic emotions; compassion, "heart".

P. 71, l. 306. *Old Exchange.*

The original "Burse" or Exchange was built by Sir Thomas Gresham in 1566-71 and destroyed by the Great Fire. The site, in the angle between Threadneedle Street and Cornhill, was occupied by a second Royal Exchange, built in 1667-69 and consisting of a quadrangle with a cloister running around the interior of the building. Above this was a corridor divided into stalls which formed a kind of bazaar.

P. 72, l. 313. *blasting.*

Withering or shriveling.

P. 72, l. 329. *Scotch Cloath.*

A cheap textile resembling lawn, but cheaper; said to have been made of nettle fiber.

P. 72, l. 333. *Conventicles.*

Religious meetings or services held by Dissenters. The word is accented *conventic'le* in seventeenth-century verse (Shakespeare, Beaumont and Fletcher, Daniel, Butler, Dryden) and is often the occasion for innuendo, as in *Hudibras* I, Canto ii, 437:

> He us'd to lay about and stickle,
> Like *Ram* or *Bull,* at *Conventicle*:

P. 73, l. 367. *pickeere.*

To skirmish playfully or amorously; to flirt. Cf. Vanbrugh, *The Relapse* (1697), III, ii:

"... to my certain knowledge your Husband is a pickering elsewhere."

P. 73, l. 369. *Miss, and Mass.*

Missal and Mass-Book (?)

P. 73, l. 370. *Reformade.*

A reformado was an officer of a disbanded company who retained his rank and received half or full pay, though he was without command. Cf. Jonson, *Every Man in His Humour,* III, v, 19-23. Here there is also a pun on the meaning of "reformed" as there is in *Epicoene,* V, ii, 67-69:

"... his Knights *reformados* are wound up as high, and insolent, as ever they were."

P. 73, l. 371. *Cully.*

A dupe, a gull.

P. 73, l. 372. *husses.*

A variant spelling of *hussies.*

P. 73, l. 382. *Broad peice.*

According to the *N.E.D.,* "A name applied after the introduction of the guinea in 1663 to the 'Unite' or 20-shilling piece ('Jacobus' and

'Carolus') of the preceding reigns, which were much broader and thinner than the new milled coinage."

P. 74, l. 394. *Cheney*.

China. The *N.E.D.* quotes the line in which this variant spelling occurs.

5. *Act II*

P. 75, l. 43. *Broad Seal*.

The Great Seal of England.

P. 76, l. 62. *Black Arts*.

Magic, necromancy.

P. 76, l. 66. *Proctors*.

Two officers of a University, appointed annually, concerned with the giving of examinations, the conferring of degrees, and the punishment of infractions of discipline.

P. 77, l. 104. *Nutmeg o' comfort*.

Cf. Elyot, *Castel of Helth* (1541), p. 31:

"Nutmigges with their swete odour comforte and dissolue . . . ." (*N.E.D.*)

P. 77, ll. 112-13. *Guitarre o' the Town*.

The *N.E.D.* cites *Sir Courtly Nice* for this figurative usage of the word *guitar,* first mentioned in 1621 in Jonson's *Gipsies Metamorphosed*.

P. 77, l. 118. *thrumble*.

Derived from *thrum* in the sense of *strum*; cf. Wycherley, *The Country Wife,* I, i:

"awkward thrumming upon the lute."

P. 77, l. 127. *Hector*.

A bully.

P. 79, l. 167. *Mair-maids*.

Mermaids.

P. 79, l. 171. *Bird.*

Child, girl, maiden. Here used as a term of opprobrium.

P. 79, l. 193. *the whimsey.*

Impulse. Cf. Tom Brown, *Amusements Serious and Comical,* p. 10:
"A whimsy takes me in the head to carry this stranger all over the town with me . . . ."

P. 80, l. 220. *Plackets.*

Aprons or petticoats. The *N.E.D.* cites this passage.

P. 80, ll. 223-24. *Mercat-cross.*

Market Cross, a cross erected in the center of a marketplace or public square.

P. 82, l. 271. *Jade.*

Worthless horse. A term of reprobation, it was also used playfully, like *jinx* or *hussy.*

P. 82, l. 274. *Malapert Boy.*

Presumptuous, impudent, saucy. Cf. Shakespeare, *Twelfth Night,* IV, i, 42:
"*Sir Toby* . . . Nay then I must have an ounce or two of this malapert blood from you."

P. 82, ll. 278-79. *Tom-Fool.*

A quasi-proper name for a dullard.

P. 82, l. 290. *half Horse.*

A centaur. Cf. Sandys's translation of Ovid, *Metamorphoses,* II, 38: "It pleas'd the Halfe-horse to be so imploy'd." (*N.E.D.*)

P. 83, l. 311. *Criss Cross.*

Christ Cross row. The alphabet, so called from the figure of a cross prefixed to it in horn-books.

P. 83, l. 335. *Maggots.*

See note to P. 106, ll. 10-11.

P. 83, l. 336. *Porridge-pots.*

Porridge-pots were distinguished for wide mouths. *Porridge* was also used figuratively to denote a conglomeration, a hodge-podge, worthless stuff.

P. 84, l. 337. *Divine Right of Presbitery.*

A parody of the phrase Divine Right of Kings.

P. 84, l. 339. *make a Conscience.*

To make something a matter of conscience, to have scruples.

P. 84, l. 355. *don't Godfrey me.*

Don't strangle me. This is a reference to the strangulation of Sir Edmund Berry Godfrey, a well-known justice of the peace, under mysterious circumstances in October, 1678. Godfrey's death was popularly blamed upon the Catholics as revenge for Titus Oates's depositions against them in the matter of the Popish Plot. Oates himself was suspected by others of assassinating Godfrey.

P. 84, l. 358. *Bear-Garden.*

A place originally set apart for the baiting of bears and used for other rough sports. William Henry Irving states in *John Gay's London* (1928), p. 294, "There were three Bear-gardens in the time of Queen Anne, one in Hockley, Clerkenwell, one in Marrybone Fields, at the back of Soho Square, and one in Tuttle (Tothill) Fields, Westminster." H. B. Wheatley in *London Past and Present* (1891), p. 137, notes that "from a very early date there was a royal garden for bear and bull baiting on the Bankside, Southwark".

P. 85, ll. 376-77. *narrow Conscience ... room for a ... Commonwealth.*

The *N.E.D.* quotes an excerpt from Giovanni Torriano, *Proverbial Phrases* (1666): "The English say, to have a wide conscience, as one may swing a cat in't."

P. 86, l. 415. *prick-ears.*

Figuratively, ears conspicuous for standing out, the ears of a person with a short haircut, a "Roundhead". The *N.E.D.* cites this usage.

P. 88, l. 478. *Bombast.*

Cotton-wool used as padding or stuffing for clothes, hence, any padding or elaboration. This passage is cited by the *N.E.D.*

P. 88, ll. 497-98. *Fortune is as fond of ... Fools.*

Cf. Wycherley, *The Gentleman Dancing-Master,* III, i:
"*Hip.* Fools have fortune, they say, indeed.
Mons. So say old *Seneque.*"

6. *Act III*

P. 90, l. 57. *Bon mine.*

Pleasant mien. Also spelled *meen* and *Meine.*

P. 90, l. 67. *Mechanick.*

Used contemptuously of a person employed in a manual occupation. Cf. Etherege, *Sir Fopling Flutter,* IV, 245:

"Writing Madam's a Mechanick part of Witt! A Gentleman should never go beyond a Song or a Billet."

P. 90, l. 69. *Haberdasher.*

Here, a dealer in small articles such as thread, tape, ribbons.

P. 91, l. 91. *divertising.*

Amusing, diverting.

P. 91, l. 102. *the Kings Box.*

When the king was not present at the play, seats in the Royal Box might be sold to others, who coveted the conspicuous places. Cf. Etherege, *Sir Fopling Flutter,* I, i, 54-55:

". . . she may look sparkishly in the Fore Front of the Kings Box, at an old Play."

P. 93, l. 154. *Sauce for a Woodcock.*

The woodcock was supposed to have no brains, and *woodcock* became a slang term for a simpleton. Cf. Shakespeare, *The Taming of the Shrew,* I, ii, 158:

"O this woodcock, what an ass it is!"

Pp. 93-94, ll. 177-78. *Court Card.*

A face card. In old slang, a gay, fluttering fellow. The *N.E.D.* quotes the *Dictionary of the Canting Crew,* 1700.

P. 94, l. 178. *Pam at Lantereloo.*

Pam, in French *Pamphile,* is the knave of clubs. Lantereloo and its descendant, loo, were fashionable card games frequently mentioned in literature in which the knave of clubs was high card. Cf. Pope, *The Rape of the Lock,* III, 61:

> "Ev'n mighty *Pam*, that Kings and Queens o'erthrew,
> And mow'd down Armies in the Fights of Lu . . ."

P. 96, l. 278. *Effigies.*

The *N.E.D.* gives this form as the original of *effigy,* and the meaning as any likeness, image, or portrait. Cf. Tom Brown, *Amusements Serious and Comical,* p. 113:

". . . the Earl of Exeter lies covered with marble, with his own effigies and his first wife's . . . ."

P. 97, l. 295. *Errant.*

Errand. This variant is also found in Etherege, *Sir Fopling Flutter,* IV, 8.

P. 97, ll. 319-20. *Flim flam.*

A flam is a cheat or swindle. Cf. Brown, *Letters From the Dead to the Living,* p. 243:

"flim-flams invented by the crafty."

P. 98, l. 353. *Fire-fork.*

A fork-shaped instrument used for stirring up the fire, putting on fuel, etc. This passage is cited by the *N.E.D.* as a figurative usage.

P. 98, l. 356.   *rotten rump . . . Roasted.*

The Rump Parliament is a name given to the remnant of the Long Parliament (restored in May, 1659) which was dissolved by Monk in February, 1660. At the fall of the Rump Parliament there was great jubilation in London, and bonfires were lighted at street corners, over which rumps of mutton and beef were roasted in mock-ceremony. Cf. Mrs. Lucy Hutchinson, *Memoirs of Colonel Hutchinson* (1638), 116.

P. 99, l. 379. *Oaths of Allegiance and Supremacy.*

The Oaths provided that the subject be "true and faithful to the King and his heirs". The Statutes of Charles II also required the Oath of Abjuration, which in practice kept Catholics and dissenters out of public office.

P. 101, l. 448. *Mandarine.*

A generic name for all grades of Chinese officials. The *N.E.D.* cites this passage.

P. 101, l. 449. *Bantammers.*

Cf. the *Loyal Protestant,* May 18, 1682, as quoted in Sybil Rosenfeld, "Restoration Stage in Newspapers and Journal, 1660-1700," *MLR,* XXX (1935), 448:

". . .This day his Excellency the Embassador from the Great King of Bantam came to our Theatre, to divert himself at a Play, attended by a numerous Train of his own Servants; who (as a Guard to his Person) preceded his Coach, arm'd with Jav'lins and Lances, some of them bearing up 2 Umbrellas of State."

P. 104, l. 565. *Cogname.*

Surname, from *cognomen.* This usage is cited by the *N.E.D.*

P. 105, ll. 575-78. *West-Smithfield . . . Westminster.*

Westminster extends to Kensington and Chelsea westward, to Temple Bar eastward, to the Thames southward, and to Marylebone northward. Smithfield was a famous horse-market. Cf. the proverb:

"Who goes to Westminster for a wife, to Paul's for a man, and to Smithfield for a horse may meet with a whore, a knave, and a jade."

7. *Act IV*

P. 106, l. 4. *Engines.*

Ingenious schemes.

P. 106, ll. 10-11. *scarify him, and take out his Worm.*

To scarify is to make an incision. *Worm* or *maggot* (see p. 83, l. 335) is a passion, a whim, a streak of madness.

P. 107, l. 37. *Fools Coat.*

Traditionally, the fool or jester wore "motley" or a coat of many colors.

P. 108, ll. 53-54. *as . . . fortified as a Low Country Town.*

Cf. Brown, *Amusements Serious and Comical,* p. 198:

"for the toping men in all professions are protected by their gravity, as the towns in Holland are by the mud and dirt about them."

P. 108, l. 71. *condemn'd to Transportation.*

Political prisoners, paupers, and felons were sometimes exiled to the colonies in lieu of punishment at home. As early as 1670 Virginia had passed an act prohibiting the importation of convicts.

P. 109, l. 96. *Hogo.*

The *N.E.D.,* which cites this figurative usage, gives one meaning of the word (*haut gout*) as "a 'high' or putrescent flavour; an offensive taste or smell." Cf. Wycherley, *Love in a Wood,* II, i:

"Moreover she is bow-legged, hopper-hipped . . . has a complexion like a Holland cheese, and no more teeth left than such as give a *haut gout* to her breath; but she is rich, faith and troth."

P. 109, l. 121. *A lack a day.*

Woe the day.

P. 111, l. 191. *Oh shad!*

As a term of abuse, cf. Jonson, *The Alchemist*, IV, vii, 45-46:
"Then you are an *Otter*, and a *Shad*, a *Whit*, A very *Tim*."

P. 112, ll. 193-94. *too high too low, like a Sowgelders Horn.*

References to the penetrating noise of the horn, sounded to announce the gelder's arrival at a place, are frequent in literature. Cf. Brown, *Letters from the Dead to the Living,* p. 306:
". . . he dreads a poet, as much as dogs do a sow-gelder."

P. 112, l. 196. *Forty One.*

1641 was the date of the Grand Remonstrance and Petition to Charles I, the beginning of rebellion.

P. 118, l. 402. *Nickumpoop.*

Nincompoop. The word is of obscure origin; early forms do not bear out Johnson's suggestion that it was a corruption of *non compos (mentis).* The *N.E.D.* cites this unusual spelling.

P. 118, ll. 405-6. *plead'st thy Face, as Whores do their Bellys.*

A female criminal who was pregnant could not be executed. Cf. Gay, *The Beggar's Opera,* I, i:
"*Peach.* Why, she may plead her belly at worst; to my knowledge she hath taken care of that security."

P. 119, l. 438. *Diaper Napkin.*

Diaper is the name of a textile, usually a linen and cotton mixture, woven with a small and simple pattern.

P. 119, l. 451. *Barn-Elms.*

A well-known dueling place in the eastern part of Barnes, adjacent to Putney. It was here that the Duke of Buckingham fatally wounded the Earl of Shrewsbury in January, 1668. Cf. Pepys, *Diary*, 17 January, 1667/68.

P. 119, l. 453. *a Squirt.*

A small tubular instrument by which water may be squirted, a kind of syringe. The *N.E.D.* quotes Feuillerat, *Revels of Edward VI*, 107:
"vj great woodden squertes by him turned and made for the combat of the lord of misrule."

P. 119, l. 464. *confin'd upon the Guard, among Tobacco takers.*

The *N.E.D.* indicates that *Guard* here is a shortening of *Guard-room* or *Guardhouse*, but there are no clues to the remainder of the passage.

P. 120, l. 489. *Fly-boats.*

Fast sailing vessels. The derivation is from the Dutch *vlieboot,* a vessel used on the *Vlie,* or channel leading out of the Zuyder Zee.

8. *Act V*

P. 125, l. 41. *the Mogul.*

The common designation among Europeans of the emperor of Delhi, whose empire at one time included most of Hindustan; the last nominal emperor was dethroned in 1857. (*N.E.D.*) By transference, any oriental potentate.

P. 128, l. 149. *Fubs.*

A term of endearment, meaning a small, chubby person. *Fubs* was a nickname given the Duchess of Portsmouth by Charles II.

P. 131, l. 247. *Vizard.*

A vizard was a mask, and by extension, a woman wearing such a mask to avoid recognition in public. The word became synonymous with *prostitute.*

P. 132, l. 291. *at the Parks.*

Probably St. James's Park, laid out by Charles II on the site of St. James's Hospital, Hyde Park, an old royal hunting-ground which became a racecourse under Charles I and under Charles II a promenade and drive.

P. 133, l. 310. *As I gaz'd unaware.*

According to Montague Summers (*Restoration Comedies,* p. 399) the words are "a translation of Mascarille's *Au Voleur!* in *Les Précieuses Ridicules* ... produced at the Petit-Bourbon, Paris, 18 November, 1659." The following quotations of the original song and its translation from *The Plays of Molière in French With an English Translation and Notes,* ed. A. R. Waller (1907) II, 28-29, will show the extent of Crowne's obligation to Molière:

> Oh, oh! je n'y prenais pas garde:
> Tandis que, sans songer à mal, je vous regarde.
> Votre oeil en tapinois me dérole mon cœur;
> Au voleur, au voleur, au voleur, au voleur!

> Oh! oh! oh! oh! I am quite off my guard,
> And, thinking no ill, you meet my regard.
> Slyly your eyes steal my heart right away,
> Stop thief! stop thief! stop thief! stop thief, I say.

R. G. Noyes states in his article, "Contemporary Musical Settings of the Songs in Restoration Drama", *ELH*, I (1934), 325-344, that the music was composed by Robert King, and that the song may be found in *The Theatre of Music* (1685), together with "O, be kind, my dear, be kind" (p. 144, see note) and two songs not included in the text of the play. These are "Farewell bonny Wully Craig", described as "a new Scotch Song", with music by Samuel Akeroyde, and "Ah, Phillis, why are you less *tendre*" to be sung "by a Fop newly come from France: To an old French Tune". The two later songs, with "Thou lovely Indian sea of charms", are also to be found in *Three New Songs in Sir Courtly Nice,* 1685. The words of "Ah Phillis" are by Thomas D'Urfey, and are included in *Pills to Purge Melancholy,* 1699.

P. 135, l. 408. *Forms.*

Etiquette.

P. 137, l. 464. *by Gogmagog.*

Gog is pictured by Ezekiel as leading a host of nations against the restored Israel, and as being defeated by the intervention of Jesus. (*Ezekiel* 38, ff.) Magog is a figure joined with Gog in *Revelations* 20, but "the land of Magog" is given in *Ezekiel* as the origin of Gog. Effigies of two giants, Gog and Magog, in Guildhall, London were apparently inspired by the legend in the *Recuyell des histoires de Troye* which stated that Gog and Magog were the survivors of a race of giants descended from the thirty-three wicked daughters of Diocletian; after their brethren had been slain by Brute and his companions, Gog and Magog were brought to London (Troynovant) and compelled to officiate as porters at the gate of the royal palace.

P. 139, l. 547. *Your Jack, to turn and roast you for another.*

A jack was a machine for turning the spit in roasting meat.

P. 140, l. 556. *doged.*

The *N.E.D.* gives only *dog-like, surly, persistent* as definitions. Here it also seems to mean *obscene.*

P. 141, l. 602. *Cotqueen.*

Vulgar, low. A cotquean is a housewife in a laborer's hut (cot); by extension, one who has the manners of a laborer's wife.

P. 141, l. 605. *Huffs.*

A huff is a blustering fellow, a hector, a bully.

P. 143, l. 664. *society o' Gotams.*

Men of Gotham, in Nottingham, were legendary fools. A collection of their "jests" was published in the sixteenth century under the title *Merrie Tales of the Mad Men of Gotham.* Typical of the Gothamites' foolishness is the story of their tumbling cheeses downhill to find their way to Nottingham market, and joining hands around a thornbush to shut in a cuckoo so that it would sing all the year.

P. 143, l. 666.   *Lord Wise-acre.*

The word may be derived from the German *weiss-ager,* a soothsayer or prophet. There is a story that Ben Jonson, at the *Devil* in Fleet Street, said to a country gentleman who boasted of his estates, "What care we for your dirt and clods? Where you have an acre of land, I have ten acres of wit." The landed gentleman is supposed to have retorted by calling Jonson "Good Mr. Wiseacre".

9. *Songs*

P. 144, l. 1.   *Oh, be kind.*

See note to p. 133, l. 310. The music is by Robert King. (Noyes, p. 336.)

P. 145, l. 1.   *Thou lovely Indian Sea of Charms.*

See note to p. 133, l. 310.

P. 145, l. 5.   *Jimminy.*

A variant of *Gemini,* a mild oath. Hildebrand (Grimm's *Deutsche Wörterbuch*) regards this as a corruption of *Jesu domine.* (*N.E.D.*)

10. *Epilogue*

P. 146, l. 7.   *Shante spark.*

From French *gentil,* the meaning is showy, smart, jaunty. The *N.E.D.* lists this example as the first occurrence of the word.

P. 146, l. 10.   *Exchange.*

Probably the New Exchange, on the south side of the Strand, and nearly opposite Bedford Street. According to Timbs, *Curiosities of London* (1855) "it was erected partly on the plan of the Royal Exchange, with vaults beneath, over which was an open paved arcade; and above were walks of shops, occupied by perfumers and publishers, milliners, and sempstresses." It was a favorite lounging-place with the fashionable. Cf. Etherege, *She Wou'd if She Cou'd,* Act II.

P. 146, l. 11.   *Temple Bar.*

Temple Bar was a gateway closing the entrance to the City of London; it separated the Strand from Fleet Street.

P. 146, l. 12.   *Beaugarzoon.*

Corruption of *beau garçon,* a handsome fellow, an exquisite, a fop, sometimes a gigolo. Cf. Buckingham, *The Rehearsal,* I, ii:
Bayes. . . . I am kept by another woman in the city.
Smith. How kept? for what?
Bayes. Why, for a *beau gerson.*

P. 147, l. 20.   *wheedle.*

H. F. B. Brett-Smith in the General Notes to his edition of Etherege's plays states that "at the time of [*Love In a Tub*] this [word] carried a very definite implication of swindling . . . . The shifts of the Wheedle were exposed in 1675 in a treatise of 352 pages, *Proteus Redivivus: or the Art of Wheedling, or Insinuation,* by R. H[ead], the author of *The English Rogue.*" (v. II, 304.) The reading of the passage in Crowne is open to question.

P. 147, l. 25.   *Nott.*

A play on the two meanings, embroidery knot and bond or obligation. Montague Summers's edition (p. 399) quotes Hobbes, *Leviathan* (1651):
"This was the first knot upon their liberty."

P. 147, l. 28.   *o're Chocolate.*

Cf. Tom Brown, *Amusements Serious and Comical,* p. 101:
". . . of all the products of your country she likes chocolate the best, because 'tis indulgent to lovers."

P. 147, l. 35.   *Bridges-street.*

Between Russell Street and Catharine Street. Drury Lane Theatre stood at its northeast corner. The character of the neighborhood is suggested by the following quotation from Dryden's epilogue to *King Arthur*:

> Here's one desires my Ladiship to meet
> At the kind Couch above in *Bridges-Street.*

P. 147, l. 36.   *higling.*

Close bargaining, "haggling".

P. 147, l. 42. *Cargozoon.*

From Spanish, meaning cargo. Cf. James Howell, *Letters,* I, xi:
". . . my body is but a cargozon of corrupt humours."

P. 147, l. 45. *Gallerys.*

"The upper gallery was the cheapest part of the Restoration Theatre. The middle gallery or eighteen-penny place, was largely fre-
quented by, if not entirely given up to, women of the town." (Summers,
Restoration Comedies, p. 400.)

P. 148, l. 57. *As well to profit as delight the mind.*

Horace, *Ars Poetica,* 333:

> Aut prodesse volunt aut delectare poetae
> aut simul et iucunda et idonea dicere vitae.

11. *Appendix A*

P. 150, l. 53. *Bone.*

An allusion to the ravages of syphilis.

P. 150, l. 64. *Net.*

A mesh snare for fish or birds.

P. 150, l. 67. *Masquerades.*

A group of masked dancers to whom, in Dorimant's words, "A
Fiddle . . . is a kind of Fop-call." The masquerades joined parties un-
invited. Cf. Etherege, *Sir Fopling Flutter,* IV, i, 184.

P. 150, l. 78. *Sir Sparkish.*

The "false wit" in Wycherley's *Country Wife* (1675).

P. 150, l. 84. *Pumpions.*

According to the *N.E.D.* the French word *pompon, melon,* has
undergone two anomalous transformations, first to *pompeon, pom-
pion, pumpion,* and finally to *pumkin.*

P. 151, l. 89. *Tho. Benskin.*

A Whig bookseller in London who, according to Plomer's *Dictionary of Printers and Booksellers* (pp. 30-31) was "first heard of in
1680/1 as a publisher on the Protestant side during the Popish Plot.
On March 10th he issued the first number of *The Protestant Oxford
Intelligence,* altered a month later to *The Impartiall London Intelli-*

gence; or, Occurrences Forraign and Domestick. On June 6th, 1681, the Earl of Danby moved the Court of King's Bench that Thomas Benskin, the publisher of *The Phanatick Intelligence,* might be ordered to find bail in £1,000 to answer a charge of scandal against the Earl, but the bail was fixed by the Court at £500. In the same year he issued a broadside entitled *The Vindication of . . . James, Duke of Monmouth."* He was the publisher of Aphra Behn's *The Round-Heads* and *The City Heiress.*

BIBLIOGRAPHY

Arber, Edward (ed.), *The Term Catalogues, 1668-1709* (London, 1903-06).

Avery, Emmett L., "A Tentative Calendar of Daily Theatrical Performances, 1660-1700", *Research Studies of the State College of Washington*, XIII (1945), 225-283.

——, "A Tentative Calendar of Daily Theatrical Performances in London, 1700-1701 to 1704-1705", *Publications of the Modern Language Association*, LXIII (1948), 114-180.

——, Unpublished lists of performance dates for *Sir Courtly Nice* to 1728. From *The London Stage, 1660-1800, Part II (1700-1729)*.

Bartholomew, A. T., "The Restoration Drama, III", *The Cambridge History of English Literature*, VIII, 202-223 (Cambridge, 1912).

Borgman, Albert S., *The Life and Death of William Mountfort* (Cambridge, Mass., 1935).

Boswell, Eleanore, *The Restoration Court Stage* (Cambridge, Mass., 1932).

Brenan, Gerald, *The Literature of the Spanish People from Roman Times to the Present Day* (Cambridge, 1951).

Brown, Tom, *Amusements Serious and Comical and Other Works*, ed. Arthur L. Hayward (London, 1927).

Buckingham, George Villiers, Duke of, "The Rehearsal", London, 1672, In *Three Centuries of Drama: English (1642-1700)*. Microprint.

Bullen, A. H., "John Crowne", *Dictionary of National Biography*, V, 243-245. (1908).

Cibber, Colley, *An Apology for the Life of Colley Cibber*, ed. R. W. Lowe (London, 1889).

Clark, W. S. II (ed.), *Dramatic Works of Roger Boyle, Earl of Orrery* (Cambridge, Mass., 1937).

Congreve, William, *Plays*, ed. A. C. Ewald (The Mermaid Series) (London, 1888).

Crowne, John, *The Dramatic Works*, ed. J. Maidment and W. H. Logan (Edinburgh, 1873-74).

Dennis, John, *The Critical Works*, ed. Edward Niles Hooker (Baltimore, 1939-43).

Dobrée, Bonamy, *Restoration Comedy* (Oxford, 1924).

Doran, John, "Their Majesties' Servants". *Annals of the English Stage, from Thomas Betterton to Edmund Kean* (New York, 1865).

Downes, John, *Roscius Anglicanus,* ed. Montague Summers (London, n.d.).

Dryden, John, *The Poetical Works,* ed. George R. Noyes (Boston, 1950).

Etherege, Sir George, *Works,* ed. H. F. B. Brett-Smith (Oxford, 1927).

Evelyn, John, *Diary,* ed. E. S. de Beer (Oxford, 1955).

Fujimura, Thomas H., *The Restoration Comedy of Wit* (Princeton, 1952).

Gaw, Allison, "Tuke's *Adventures of Five Hours,* in Relation to the 'Spanish Plot' and to John Dryden", *Studies in English Drama,* ed. Allison Gaw (Philadelphia, 1917).

Gay, John, "The Beggar's Opera", London, 1728, In *Three Centuries of Drama:* English *(1701-1750).* Microprint.

Gildon, Charles, *A Comparison Between the Two Stages,* ed. S. B. Wells (Princeton, 1942).

Gouldson, Kathleen, "Three Studies in Golden Age Drama", *Spanish Golden Age Poetry and Drama,* ed. Allison Peers (Liverpool, 1946).

Herrick, Robert, *Poetical Works,* ed. L. C. Martin (Oxford, 1936).

Howell, James, *Epistolae Ho-Elianae,* ed. Joseph Jacobs (London, 1892).

Hughes, Leo, *A Century of English Farce* (Princeton, 1956).

Hutchinson, Mrs. Lucy, *Memoirs of the Life of Colonel Hutchinson,* ed. the Rev. Julius Hutchinson. Revised with notes by C. H. Firth (London, 1906).

Jonson, Ben, *Works,* ed. C. H. Herford and Percy Simpson (Oxford, 1925-52).

Kronenberger, Louis, *The Thread of Laughter* (New York, 1952).

Langbaine, Gerard, *An Account of the English Dramatick Poets* (Oxford, 1691).

Loftis, John, "Spanish Drama in Neoclassical England", *Comparative Literature,* XI (1959), 29-34.

Lynch, Kathleen, *The Social Mode of Restoration Comedy* (New York, 1926).

Moreto, Agustín, "No Puede Ser el Guardar una Mujer", In *Biblioteca de Autores Españoles,* XXXIX, 187-208.

Noyes, R. G., *Ben Jonson on the English Stage (1660-1776)* (Cambridge, Mass., 1935).

——, "Contemporary Musical Settings of the Songs in Restoration Drama", *English Literary History,* I (1934), 325-344.

——, "Mrs. Bracegirdle's Acting in Crowne's *Justice Busy*", *Modern Language Notes,* XLIII (1928), 390-391.

Pedicord, John, *The Theatrical Public in the Time of Garrick* (New York, 1954).

Plomer, Henry R., *A Dictionary of the Printers and Booksellers Who Were at Work in England, Scotland, and Ireland from 1668 to 1725,* ed. Arundell Esdaile (Publications of the Bibliographical Society) (London, 1922).

Pope, Alexander, *The Poems,* ed. John Butt. The Twickenham Edition (New Haven, 1939-54).

Preston, John, *Genuine Letters from a Gentleman to a Young Lady His Pupil,* ed. Thomas Hull (London, 1772).

Rennert, Hugo A., *The Spanish Stage in the Time of Lope de Vega* (New York, 1909).

Rochester, John Wilmot, Earl of, *Poems,* ed. Vivian de Sola Pinto (London, 1953).

Rosenfeld, Sybil, "Restoration Stage in Newspapers and Journal, 1660-1700", *Modern Language Review,* XXX (1935), 445-459.

——, *Strolling Players and Drama in the Provinces (1660-1765)* (Cambridge, 1939).

Schevill, Rudolph, *The Dramatic Art of Lope de Vega* (Berkeley, 1918).

Shakespeare, William, *Works,* ed. Sir Arthur Quiller-Couch and John Dover Wilson (Cambridge, 1921-57).

Smith, John Harrington, *The Gay Couple in Restoration Comedy* (Cambridge, Mass., 1948).

Summers, Montague, *The Playhouse of Pepys* (London, 1935).

——, *Restoration Comedies* (Boston, 1922).

——, *The Restoration Theatre* (New York, 1934).

Timbs, John, *Curiosities of London* (London, 1855).

Vanbrugh, Sir John, *Plays,* ed. A. E. H. Swain (The Mermaid Series) (New York, 1949).

Vega Carpio, Lope Felix de, *El mayor imposible,* ed. John Brooks (Tucson, Ariz., 1934).

Waller, A. R. (ed.), *The Plays of Molière in French With an English Translation and Notes* (Edinburgh, 1907).

Ward, A. W., *History of English Dramatic Literature to the Death of Queen Anne.* Revised (London, 1899).

Wheatley, H. B., *London Past and Present* (London, 1891).

White, Arthur F., "John Crowne and America", *Publications of the Modern Language Association,* XXXV (1920), 447-463.

——, *John Crowne: His Life and Dramatic Works* (Cleveland, 1922).

Whiting, G. W., "Political Satire in London Stage Plays, 1680-1683", *Modern Philology,* XXVIII (1930), 29-43.

Winship, George Parker, *A Bibliography of the Restoration Dramatist, John Crowne* (Cambridge, Mass., 1922).

Wycherley, William, *Plays,* ed. W. C. Ward (The Mermaid Series) (London, n.d.).